The MONOCLE
Travel Guide Series

Rio de Janeiro

For more information, please visit *gestalten.com*
———
Bibliographic information published by the Deutsche Nationalbibliothek: The Deutsche Nationalbibliothek lists this publication in the Deutsche National-bibliografie; detailed bibliographic data are available online at *dnb.d-nb.de*

This book was printed on paper certified by the FSC®

Monocle editor in chief: *Tyler Brûlé*
Monocle editor: *Andrew Tuck*
Series editor: *Joe Pickard*
Guide editor: *Matt Alagiah*
———
Designed by *Monocle*
Proofreading by *Monocle*
Typeset in *Plantin & Helvetica*
———
Printed by *Offsetdruckerei Grammlich, Pliezhausen*

Made in Germany

Published by *Gestalten*, Berlin 2016
ISBN 978-3-89955-634-6

Welcome
—— Paradise by the book

The first thing that strikes a visitor to *Rio de Janeiro* is the city's staggering natural beauty. Denizens of Rio, or Cariocas, have named their hometown the *Cidade Maravilhosa* (Marvellous City). Anywhere else this might seem conceited but here it is, if anything, understated. Even with its built-up coastline and urban sprawl, looking along *Ipanema Beach* towards the Dois Irmãos mountains you still feel like an explorer discovering a *tropical paradise*.

No city is more defined by its beaches and no beaches have become so synonymous with a city, from Mario Testino's photographs of *bronzed bodies* on Copacabana to the globally familiar lilt of "The Girl from Ipanema". Meanwhile, the *Parque Nacional da Tijuca* urban forest strives to reclaim the city, creating canopied pockets of *lush vegetation* that perfectly balance all that bleached sand.

But there's more to Rio than its looks. It has a rich and *colourful past* told in the *architecture* of the city, from Portuguese colonial-era townhouses to the modernism of *Oscar Niemeyer* masterpieces. Around the city you'll also find world-class *cultural institutions*, from museums and galleries to music venues blasting out live *samba*.

Then there are the *Cariocas*, as easy-going and *fun-loving* as their stereotype. Join the masses at *Carnival* or for a *caipirinha* in Baixo Gávea on a Thursday evening, or wander up the winding streets of Santa Teresa for a *hearty feijoada* and you'll always be greeted with open arms.

Rio is a gorgeous city full of gorgeous people but there's a lot below the surface. Read on to uncover its hidden depths. — (M)

Contents
—— Navigating the city

Use the key below to help navigate the guide section by section.

 Hotels

 Food and drink

 Beach business

R Retail

T Things we'd buy

E Essays

C Culture

D Design and architecture

S Sport and fitness

W Walks

Map
—— The city at a glance

Rio is broadly divided into four zones: Zona Sul, Zona Oeste, Zona Norte and Centro. Although most of the famous beaches (and the majority of the recommendations in this guide) are located in Zona Sul and Centro, you should venture out to the other districts.

The city's roots are in downtown in Centro, where you'll find cobbled streets and colonial townhouses that resemble the heart of Lisbon. The poorer Zona Norte is home to most of Rio's favelas and is often missed by visitors – but this is the birthplace of samba and home to the Maracanã Stadium, so it deserves a place in your itinerary.

Zona Sul is Rio's most affluent area, containing Ipanema, Copacabana, Lagoa and Botafogo, and it's where you'll find the city's best hotels, restaurants and shops. However, in recent decades the city has expanded out to the Zona Oeste, where there's Barra da Tijuca and the Olympic Park. This is an area of large developments, apartment complexes and shopping malls, as well as seemingly endless stretches of pristine beach.

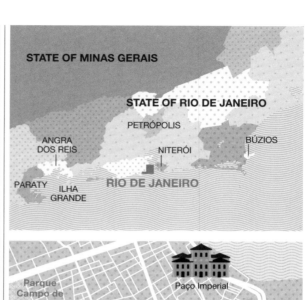

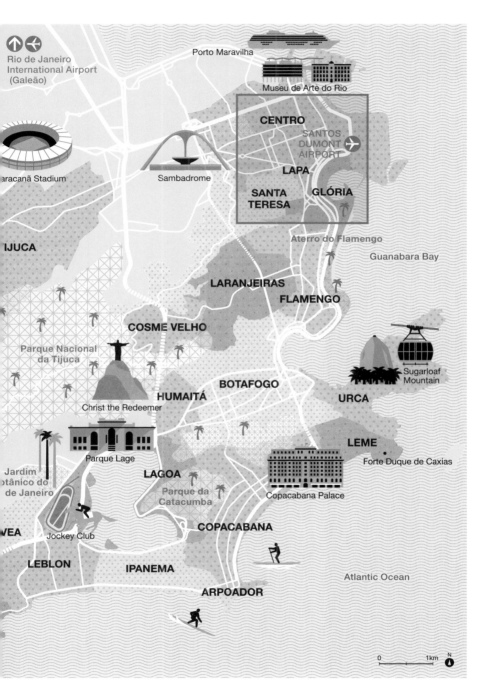

Rio de Janeiro
International Airport
(Galeão)

Porto Maravilha

Museu de Arte do Rio

CENTRO

SANTOS
DUMONT
AIRPORT

LAPA

Maracanã Stadium

Sambadrome

SANTA
TERESA

GLÓRIA

Aterro do Flamengo

Guanabara Bay

IJUCA

LARANJEIRAS

FLAMENGO

COSME VELHO

Parque Nacional
da Tijuca

BOTAFOGO

Sugarloaf
Mountain

HUMAITÁ

URCA

Christ the Redeemer

LEME

Parque Lage

Forte Duque de Caxias

Jardim
Botânico do
de Janeiro

LAGOA

Parque da
Catacumba

Copacabana Palace

VEA

Jockey Club

COPACABANA

LEBLON

IPANEMA

Atlantic Ocean

ARPOADOR

0   1km   N

Need to know
—— Get to grips with the basics

Whether to kiss or not to kiss at first introduction, which section of the beach to choose to lay your towel on and how to drink those oh-so-big bottles of beer: here are some quick facts that might come in handy when visiting Rio for the first time.

Respect the rules
Transport

Rio's public-transport system – admittedly still a work in progress – has an etiquette all of its own. There are designated seats for people who are disabled, pregnant, over the age of 60 or who have young children. If you are seated in one of these on a crowded bus, metro or BRT it's important to give it up if someone from one of the above categories comes aboard. Otherwise you'll be greeted with scowls.

On the metro there are women-only carriages during morning and evening rush hour, clearly marked in pink with signs that say *carro exclusivo para mulheres*. If you're a man don't cheekily try to get on one of these carriages at the wrong time: you will be pushed off.

On buses it's cash only and you should try to carry R$10 notes or less. The same applies when taking taxis: drivers rarely have change and it's even less common for them to accept cards.

Many taxi drivers don't like picking people up from the beach. Make sure you are completely dry and dusted of sand then walk a few blocks away to hail one.

I'm out of tobacco. Will sand do?

When in Rio
Safety

When asked about safety in the city, any local will be quick to say that you should be fine – as long as you are *esperto* ("street-smart").

Most incidents in Zona Sul (the main tourist area) come down to petty crime so the best way to stay safe is to carry as few precious items on you as possible: some change and a credit card should be enough. Leave all jewellery or watches behind in your hotel and avoid wearing flashy, expensive items of clothing. People in Rio are very casual and you don't want to stand out as a gringo.

At night avoid walking down empty or poorly lit streets. There are plenty of routes with lots of commercial hustle and bustle so stick to those. Finally, don't walk around talking on your mobile phone.

First past the post
Beaches

The city's beaches are broken down into sections according to numbered *postos* (posts), each of which offers a different atmosphere.

Copacabana tends to be more democratic and the boundaries less defined: anyone and everyone can be found on these golden sands come Sunday.

Ipanema and Leblon have clearer sections. Arpoador, in-between Copacabana and Ipanema, is frequented by surfers. Posto 8.5, in front of Rua Farme de Amoedo (known as Bolsa de Valores or Crystal Palace), is the gay section. Posto 9, at the end of

Rua Vinícius de Moraes, is the Garota de Ipanema (Girl from Ipanema) beach and tends to be the best spot to find tanned and toned bodies. Beyond Posto 10 in Leblon is the place for those who love sports: football, volleyball and *frescobol* (two-person paddle ball) games are ubiquitous.

North-south divide
Districts

Rio is divided along social, economic and racial lines: it can feel like two completely different places. Zona Sul is associated with upper-class, affluent Brazilians and Zona Norte is commonly seen as a dangerous no-go area, home to the majority of the city's estimated 1,000 favelas.

Zona Sul is where you'll find Ipanema, Copacabana and Botafogo, as well as most of the city's tourist attractions. Zona Norte is home to all of the samba schools and the Maracanã Stadium.

New kids on the block
Property

New apartment blocks are going up and up in older neighbourhoods as the city attempts to avoid greater sprawl west. Rio's port region is being revitalised with the aim of increasing density. Botafogo is also experiencing growth as a number of its buildings are being ripped down and replaced.

Even some favelas are proving attractive to developers. Properties in Vidigal and Babilônia in Zona Sul have been bought up by foreigners seeking to start businesses there, which has driven up prices.

Make a day of it
Dining

The most important meal is lunch and it does not necessarily end with the arrival of the bill. Put aside at least two hours on weekdays then on Saturdays and Sundays be prepared: it can be a day-long event.

At most restaurants, with the exception of fine-dining establishments, reservations are rarely taken. If it's a popular spot expect queues at the weekend; for an authentic Carioca experience, hang out with a bucket of beers on the pavement while you wait for your table.

Most restaurants in Rio are closed on weekdays between 15.00 and 18.00; only *padarias* (bakeries) and *botequins* (bars) are open for snacks.

I could get used to long lunches

Cold comforts
Drinking

Wine culture is a relatively new trend in Brazil. Unless they're at a fine-dining restaurant, most Brazilians will opt for a cold caipirinha or a *chope* (an ice-cold half-pint of draft beer). If there is no *chope* on tap, *cervejas* (beers) are usually served in 600ml or 1 litre bottles to be shared.

Meet and greet
Etiquette

Brazilians are known to be quite touchy-feely. A two-kiss greeting between women or a man and a woman is normal, even on first introduction. Kiss the other person's right cheek first.

A standard greeting between men is a right-hand shake followed by a few pats on the back with your left hand. Good friends greet each other with a kiss on the right cheek followed by a big bear hug. Just extending your hand with no extra touching comes across as a little *frio* (cold) to most Cariocas.

Dress to impress
Clothing

Rio is extremely informal but don't mistake casualness for lack of style. The majority of venues will have no problem if you turn up in T-shirt, shorts and Havaianas. For a select few restaurants and nightclubs, men will need a button-down or polo shirt, trousers and closed shoes. Regardless of the season Rio gets *very* hot and humid so opt for lighter fabrics and colours.

What? I want to look the part

Hotels
—— At home in the Marvellous City

The hospitality scene in Rio has undergone something of a transformation in recent years. A decade ago there were few options filling the gap between the stately luxury of the Belmond Copacabana Palace and the cheaper end of the spectrum, which was dominated by beachfront tower blocks with hundreds of rooms. The selection today, however, is far richer and more diverse. A bed at the 89-room Fasano has become the most desirable location in town, while a crop of design-conscious boutique hotels offering a unique and highly personal service has emerged.

Much of this is down to the rehabilitation of Santa Teresa. The hillside district above Centro was once a no-go area but is now one of the hottest postcodes. Since 2004, two of the city's best hotels have opened: the Hotel Santa Teresa and Mama Ruisa. Similarly, the suburb of Barra da Tijuca has been flourishing: it too now boasts its own stable of luxury accommodation.

①
Belmond Copacabana Palace, Copacabana
Old-school glamour

The most sophisticated address in Rio has ushered the rich and famous across its marble-clad threshold since it opened its doors in 1923. Edith Piaf once serenaded guests, the king and queen of Norway have laid their heads on its pillows and the Rolling Stones used one of its long grand hallways as a makeshift running track for warming up before performing on Copacabana Beach in 2006.

The Palace's rooms (there are 239 of them) are a masterclass in quiet, simple grandeur. It also boasts the best spa facilities in Rio, a beautiful colonnaded outdoor pool (which is supervised throughout the day and night) and a smart, well-equipped gym. And that's before you appraise the food: there are two excellent restaurants, one of which, Mee, was awarded one of Latin America's first Michelin stars. It offers a pan-Asian tasting menu created by Ken Hom that pairs each course with a different saké.
Avenida Atlântica, 1702
+55 (21) 2548 7070
belmond.com/copacabana-palace
-rio-de-janeiro

MONOCLE COMMENT: The Chef's Table – tucked away in the kitchens of the Copacabana Palace's superb Cipriani restaurant – is a novel dining experience. Chef Luca Orini presents a tailored tasting menu which he brings to the table himself.

Pool service
—
An army of
assistants
cater to
guests

Grand Hyatt Rio, Barra de Tijuca
Big and beautiful

The Grand Hyatt in Rio opened
in late 2015 in the glitzy district of
Barra da Tijuca, with the Atlantic
Ocean in front and the Marapendi
lagoon behind. With 436 rooms
and suites, a spa, fitness room,
outdoor pool and two ballrooms,
it's no discreet boutique – but
interiors by Canadian firm Yabu
Pushelberg ensure it remains light
and airy.
Avenida Lucio Costa, 9600
+ 55 (11) 2838 3346
riodejaneiro.grand.hyatt.com

MONOCLE COMMENT:
Rooms feature floor-to-ceiling
windows and terraces offer epic
views of the natural landscape.

*I find that views
of Dois Irmãos are
best savoured with
a caipirinha*

Eagle eyes

Telescopes
help guests
enjoy the
views

③
Hotel Santa Teresa, Santa Teresa
Lofty sophistication

This former coffee-plantation
farmhouse was converted into a
hotel in 2008 by Frenchman
François Delort. The design makes
the most of the building's assets:
the beautiful heritage-listed brick
wall in the lobby area, for instance,
and the pitched roofs in some of
the top-floor rooms. That's not to
mention its location at the top
of a hill with breathtaking views
over the city and Guanabara Bay.

   This vista can be enjoyed
from the outdoor pool area, the
Têrèze restaurant (which serves
contemporary Brazilian-French
fusion cuisine) and Bar dos
Descasados (*see page 41*) under
the arches in the farmhouse's
old slave quarters. There is
also a spa for hotel guests.
Rua Almirante Alexandrino, 660
+55 (21) 3380 0200
santa-teresa-hotel.com

MONOCLE COMMENT: All 43
rooms are different and offer
something unique but our
pick is the Loft Suite with its
balcony, pitched roof and pair
of Diz armchairs by Sérgio
Rodrigues.

④
La Maison by Dussol, Gávea
Global escape

Just a short drive from the thrumming beaches of Ipanema and Leblon, La Maison by Dussol is a hidden gem that feels a million miles from the city rush. The hotel was beautifully restored by brothers François-Xavier (*pictured*) and Jacques Dussol in 2004. It clings to the hillside of Gávea and offers a panorama of Parque Nacional da Tijuca, the saltwater lagoon and Christ the Redeemer.

Each of the five suites has decor inspired by a different country. There's also a pool nestled in the tropical garden and while La Maison doesn't have a restaurant, the chef makes a variety of traditional and international dishes to order.
Rua Sérgio Porto, 58
+ 55 (21) 3205 3585
bydussol.com

MONOCLE COMMENT: Three of the themed rooms (Copacabana, Recamier and Tiffany) overlook the forest.

⑤
Ipanema Inn, Ipanema
Boutique by the sea

The Ipanema Inn is one of the few hotels situated right in the heart of Ipanema. Set back one street from the beach it has the benefit of being close to the sun and sand but also far enough away from the crowds.

Daniel Gorin, the manager and grandson of the original founder, had the hotel renovated in 2014. The redesign was led by renowned Brazilian architect Bel Lobo. The 56 rooms feature large windows and furniture by contemporary Brazilian designer Jader Almeida. One other perk is that you can pick up beach towels and parasols at the reception for a day of sun-worshipping.
Rua Maria Quitéria, 27
+ 55 (21) 2529 1000
ipanemainn.com.br

MONOCLE COMMENT: The Ipanema Inn also has a sister property a few minutes down the beach in Arpoador, aptly named the Arpoador Inn.

6
Fasano, Ipanema
Design-centric digs

The Fasano came about due to
an unlikely collaboration between
designer Philippe Starck and
Brazilian restaurateur and hotelier
Rogério Fasano. The result is a slick
89-room hotel with an understated
aesthetic created by good use of
natural tones and materials such as
Brazilian ironwood.

The rooms with a view down
Ipanema Beach towards Dois Irmãos
each have a pair of Sérgio Rodrigues
chairs on the balcony. There is also
a touch of Starck eccentricity and
flamboyance: rooms have multiple
large curved mirrors specially
designed by him for the hotel.

The Fasano's other assets
are the infinity rooftop pool and
its Londra bar kitted out with
mementos and paraphernalia
relating to the British capital,
Rogério's favourite city.
Avenida Vieira Souto, 80
+55 (21) 3202 4000
fasano.com.br

MONOCLE COMMENT: The Fasano's
location is second to none but only
about half of the rooms have a sea
view, so be sure to ask. There are
three Deluxe Ocean-Front Suites
and these are easily the best.

Sun worship
─
Catch some
rays on the
tiered deck

Bespoke decor
──
The hotel is furnished with one-off designs

7

Mama Ruisa, Santa Teresa
Personalised service

In 2004, when Frenchman Jean
Michel Ruis bought a 19th-century
colonial mansion that once belonged
to the Bulhões de Carvalho family,
the neighbourhood was just turning
around. This elevated part of town
had been overlooked for more than
half a century as the beachfront
districts of Copacabana and Ipanema
had their time in the sun. Ruis was
part of a wave of people bringing new
life and investment to Santa Teresa.

His is easily the nicest boutique
hotel in Rio. There are just seven
airy rooms, each themed around a
famous historic personality (Carmen
Miranda, for instance), with floor-
to-ceiling windows to capitalise on
the views.
Rua Santa Cristina, 132
+55 (21) 2508 8142
mamaruisa.com

MONOCLE COMMENT: Ruis prides
himself on giving each guest a unique
experience; he can recommend a
personalised itinerary for your visit.

It's not a monocle but it does the job

⑧
Clubhouse Rio, Ipanema
Join the club

Perched above a winding cobbled street with sweeping views across Copacabana Beach, the newly opened Clubhouse Rio is an imaginative twist on the members' club. The three elegant and cosy bedrooms (which do not require membership to book) are tucked away on the first floor of this imposing former townhouse. There are two more bedrooms at the back of the house, near the swimming pool.

The atmospheric interiors were designed by Rio-based UK designer Lizzie Crocker and are an understated mix of the reclaimed and the new; a set of old cinema seats in the reception area were found at an antiques market in the notorious Cidade de Deus (City of God) favela.

The dining room is a communal affair; the celebrated Brazilian musician Seu Jorge once gave an impromptu concert here.
Rua Saint Romain, 184
+55 (21) 3586 0456
clubhouserio.com

MONOCLE COMMENT: Chef Yann Kamps's repertoire includes light interpretations of Brazilian classics; the baked palm with béchamel sauce is a highlight.

⑨
Marina All Suites, Leblon
Sea views guaranteed

The Marina All Suites and the Marina Palace (the two were once affiliated but are now separate entities) are landmarks on the beachfront strip that encompasses both Ipanema and Leblon. When it opened in 1999 the Marina All Suites was one of the first design hotels in Rio.

Every one of the 41 suites has a sea view; a few take in views over both the beach and Christ the Redeemer. There's also a great rooftop pool with a bar. In the restaurant on the first floor, chef Lydia Gonzalez rustles up contemporary dishes with a Brazilian twist.
Avenue Delfim Moreira, 696
+55 (21) 2172 1100
marinaallsuites.com.br

MONOCLE COMMENT: This hotel is part of a group of three five-star design hotels across the country. The other two are worth considering if you're in Brazil for a longer stay: the Villa Rasa in Búzios, a fishing village where Rio's high society go for long weekends; and the Pousada Maravilha on the island of Fernando de Noronha, 350km from the mainland.

10
Casa Dois Irmãos, Santa Teresa
Fresh perspective

Canadian siblings Kristopher and Josephine Jennings-Bramly opened this two-bedroom guesthouse in 2015. When they bought it in 2008, it was little more than a cement box. They've since opened up the windows, introduced hardwood elements and built a terrace with incredible views. The communal living room on the upper floor is a lovely place to relax with a book.
Rua Doutor Julio Otoni, 419
+55 (21) 9 8103 5454
casadoisirmaos.com.br

MONOCLE COMMENT: The duo have plans to open two more bedrooms soon but for now we recommend staying in the Elizabeth Room.

11
Sheraton Grand Rio
Hotel & Resort, Vidigal
Old faithful reimagined

The Sheraton Rio sits on its own stretch of ocean frontage in Vidigal right at the end of Leblon Beach. It is something of an icon in Rio but underwent major renovations in 2014, so it feels anything but faded. The lobby now extends onto a bar with sweeping ocean panoramas best drunk in with a cocktail. There are three pools and two dining options: grilled Brazilian steaks are the speciality of the Casarão Restaurant, while more refined French cuisine is served at L'Etoile on the 26th floor. Each room has a balcony overlooking the beach.
Avenida Niemeyer, 121
+55 (21) 2529 1122
sheraton-rio.com.br

MONOCLE COMMENT: An absolute must is a sundowner at the Dry Martini Bar designed by cocktail connoisseur Javier de las Muelas. The extravagant drinks are just as good as in the Barcelona original.

12
Maria Santa Teresa, Santa Teresa
Quirky independent

German businessman Hans Georg Näder bought this townhouse as a playground for himself and his friends but then decided to convert it into a boutique hotel in May 2015.
The rooms are simple and slightly eccentric in decor: each is denoted by a playful mural of wildlife outside the door. Three of the bedrooms have balconies and guests can use antique binoculars to look at the sprawling city below. There are also communal areas in which to socialise and unwind: an open-air pool, rooftop barbecue area and cigar lounge.
Rua Aprazivel, 163
+55 (21) 3259 7169
mariasantateresa.com

MONOCLE COMMENT: The living room has been furnished with items from Näder's own collection, including a motorbike on the wall. There's also a fine collection of reading material.

⑬
Casa Mosquito, Copacabana
Bright and breezy

"The view is the big luxury here,"
says manager Rosa dos Prazeres.
And she isn't wrong: the rooftop pool
overlooks the Copacabana shoreline.
Many of the hotel's staff members
are from the Cantagalo favela that
sweeps up the nearby mountainside.
The nine bedrooms are each named
after celebrated Brazilian artists; the
Elis Regina suite has arguably the best
shower view in Rio.

Designed by Louis Planès, who
opened the hotel with his partner
Benjamin Cano in 2011, the rooms
are simple and smart; you'll discover
bold Cole & Son wallpaper hanging
on the walls and crisp Al Faira
linen on the beds.
Rua Saint Roman, 222
+55 (21) 3586 5042
casamosquito.com

MONOCLE COMMENT: Chef Celio
Farias offers a set menu each night
in the large communal dining room,
dictated by the produce picked up in
the local market.

Back to life
—
Plans are afoot to refurbish the
Hotel Nacional, a late-period
Oscar Niemeyer masterpiece
in the beach neighbourhood of
São Conrado. After decades
lying empty and abandoned, the
steel-and-glass behemoth was
bought in 2009 by businessman
Marcelo Henrique Limírio
Gonçalves.

Food and drink
—— Dining
Carioca-style

Eating out in Rio hasn't always been the most exciting experience. But that's started to change as a new wave of chefs and food-industry entrepreneurs have begun putting the city on the culinary radar.

People here enjoy their meat so vegetarians can struggle for options, although Celeiro (*see page 38*) is a good start. Cariocas also have a longstanding love affair with Asian cuisine; Brazil has one of the world's largest populations of people of Japanese descent. This is married with the country's extensive bounty of fresh fruit, vegetables and seafood for a deliciously tropical interpretation.

Service might seem slow and confused at times (especially if you are used to London or New York standards) but staff are – almost without exception – friendly. Try to meet them with good humour and you won't be disappointed.

Restaurants and bars are open late and reservations are rarely required. If you do have a bit of a wait, a cold *chope* and some finger food will see you through.

Restaurants
Where to eat

① JoJo, Jardim Botânico
Neighbourhood favourite

Joana Carvalho (known as Jojo) set up this charming bistro on quiet Rua Pacheco Leão in Jardim Botânico in 2011. There are just 14 tables here, all on the pavement; in the evening candles on each create a welcoming and romantic atmosphere. And when it's cold (admittedly rare in Rio), a blanket is laid on the back of each chair.

Jojo's kitchen is miniscule but the cooks turn out excellent dishes. We recommend ordering two plates of bruschetta to start: one with brie, honey and truffle oil; the other with lashings of mushroom ragú and Parma ham. Then try Jojo's take on Bahian speciality *muquequinha*, which combines white fish, *farofa (see box, page 32)*, traditional spices and rice. Every Thursday, Jojo orders 25 dozen oysters from the southern state of Santa Catarina and holds an "oyster hour" from 19.00.
Rua Pacheco Leão, 812
+55 (21) 3565 9007
jojocafe.com.br

Breakfast

01 **Da Casa da Táta, Gávea:** This small and buzzy spot serves a delicious Brazilian breakfast of cake, bread, fruit and coffee that will comfort weary travellers. *dacasadatata.com.br*

02 **Empório Jardim, Jardim Botânico:** There's no set menu so you can mix and match your morning favourites into a breakfast combo. There is wi-fi and every table has a plug, making it a great place to catch up with work emails (if you must). *emporiojardimrio.com.br*

03 **Talho Capixaba, Leblon:** What started out as a butcher shop in the 1960s has expanded over the years into a complete deli with a bakery, patisserie and wine cellar. It's where locals come to restock the gourmet items in their fridges and there is always a queue to eat-in – but the breakfast is worth the wait. *talhocapixaba.com.br*

Culinary all stars

Directly opposite on Rua Dias Ferreira are two more restaurants run by the Sushi Leblon folk: Zuka, an elegant space with chef Ludmilla Soeiro at the helm (try the grilled heart of palm), and Brigite's, which has a lighter menu and plenty of vegetarian options. *zuka.com.br; brigites.com.br*

2
Sushi Leblon, Leblon
Japanese with a twist

"She'll never stop working. She's obsessed!" says Sushi Leblon's manager Bianca Gayoso of her mother, Ana Carolina (*pictured, left*), who opened Sushi Leblon in 1986 with her late husband: hang-gliding world champion Pepê.

The sleek dining room is frequented by locals (including the odd movie star) who come to dine on specialities such as *sushi de agulhão branco* (butterfish and fried quail egg nigiri with truffle oil) and tuna tartare, all served on crockery by São Paulo-based Japanese potters Hideko Honma and Kimi Nii.
Rua Dias Ferreira, 256
+55 (21) 2512 7830
sushileblon.com

Little Italy
—
There are four Gero restaurants in Brazil

③

Gero, Ipanema
Old-school Italian

When hotelier Rogério Fasano opened Gero in 2002 he raised the gastronomic bar for the whole city. The restaurant is consistently outstanding and has built up a loyal clientele. The menu is heavy on classic Italian staples such as lamb shanks and veal ravioli; our top picks are the saffron risotto with ossobuco and the crushed potato with goat's cheese and egg yolk.

The interior was designed by Aurélio Martinez Flores and features exposed-brick walls and a wonderful indoor tree.
Rua Anibal de Mendonça, 157
+ 55 (21) 2239 8158
fasano.com.br

④
Azumi, Copacabana
Straight from the sea

The squeamish seated at Azumi's
counter might want to look away as
the sushi chefs prepare *cavaquinha
ceviche* from live brown-shelled
lobsters native to Brazil. The resulting
paper-thin slices, like the rest of the
no-frills menu of classic Japanese
fare, are a mouthwatering treat.
The restaurant was opened in 1989
by husband-and-wife team Isao and
Yumiko O'Hara and is now run by
their daughter Alyssa.
Rua Ministro Viveiros de Castro, 127
+55 (21) 2541 4294

⑤
Formidable, Leblon
French connection

This is the new bistro from the
team behind popular Botafogo
haunt Irajá, headed by chef Pedro
de Artagão. Service and atmosphere
in both is informal and relaxed;
food unfussy but assured. But while
Irajá serves contemporary Brazilian
cuisine, Formidable – as the name
perhaps suggests – is inspired by
French cookery. Here you can enjoy
an entrée of *steak tartare maison*
followed by *côte de boeuf et frites* with
profiteroles to finish. *Et pourquoi pas?*
Rua João Lira, 148
+55 (21) 2239 7632
formidablebistrot.com.br

⑥
La Bicyclette, Jardim Botânico
Pedal power

If it weren't for the surrounding
greenery, you might think you were in
a Paris boulangerie. Henri Forcellino,
the Frenchman behind the crunchy
baguettes served here, was a
bread-making hobbyist when he
started delivering homemade goods
by bicycle. When demand grew,
Forcellino and his wife Ana Paula
Gentil opened La Bicyclette in 2010
in the heart of the Jardim Botânico
neighbourhood and a second outpost
inside the garden itself in 2012.

Perfect for a slow-paced breakfast,
the menu is à la French; think *oeuf à
la coque*, croque monsieur and
campagne bread. The secret to their
success is not too different from that
of good bread, says Forcellino:
"The right ingredients, patience
and respect for natural processes
at a slow and steady pace, like
that of a bicycle."
Espaço Tom Jobim
Rua Jardim Botânico, 1008
+55 (21) 3594 2589
labicyclette.com.br

⑦
Bar Lagoa, Ipanema
Old-school service

Few places in Rio have as much heritage as this 1934 art deco establishment overlooking the lagoon. Originally called Bar Berlim, the place used to cater to the community of German immigrants who would come in for Bavarian food and music. While the music balcony is no longer in use, the schnitzel and potato salad are still house favourites.

Little has changed since the restaurant's opening: the interiors are original and the walls still feature the marble shipped from Italy in the 1930s.

A reputation for cranky waitstaff (many of whom have worked here for more than 40 years) has become part of the experience. The curt service is in good fun; the waiters are still attentive and ensure you always have an ice-cold *chope* in hand.

Avenida Epitácio Pessoa, 1674
+55 (21) 2523 1135
barlagoa.com.br

I've taste-tested three dishes already but best try one more

⑧
Bira de Guaratiba, Barra de Guaratiba
Bayside escape

If you need a break from the city centre, this is the perfect place. Its vista over Restinga da Marambaia bay alone makes the one-hour drive from Ipanema worth it (but beware you don't get caught in traffic). The traditional selection of dishes shows the best Brazil has to offer, from octopus risotto and *farofa* (*see box, page 32*) to the freshest seafood. But it's the green space that makes this one of Rio's most treasured establishments – it feels as if you're dining at the top of a treehouse.

Estrada da Vendinha, 68A
+55 (21) 2410 8304
restaurantedobira.com.br

Outdoor food markets

Visiting an outdoor food market in Rio, or *feira livre* as they are known, is a unique and wonderfully sensorial experience. You can buy everything from fresh seafood and meat to vegetables, fruits, nuts, spices and flowers.

Every day of the week from early morning until lunchtime a specific street or square around the city is home to several produce stands. Vendors sell their harvest by chanting what is on offer, creating a cacophony of musical calls.

You'll be encouraged to try samples as you walk along. Don't shy away from these; it's a great way to introduce yourself to unfamiliar produce. Vendors also set up stands with typical food from around the country to eat on the go. Here are some of our favourite *feiras* and ideas for what you should purchase.

01 Bairro Peixoto market, Copacabana: Try native fruits such as *jabuticaba* and *graviola* at this open-air market. *Wednesday*

02 Antero de Quental market, Leblon: Head here for the finest organic fruit and vegetables. *Thursday*

03 Santos Dumont Square market, Baixo Gávea: For *pastel de feira* (stuffed pasties) – and don't miss the strawberries when they are in season. *Friday*

04 Rua Frei Leandro Market, Jardim Botânico: The best tapioca and *coalho* cheese crêpes. Also keep an eye out for bowls of fresh açaí berries from the Amazon. *Saturday*

Paws aren't the best tools – luckily I'm a burger-eating expert

⑨
T T Burger, Arpoador
Burgers with bang

The lunchtime queues often stretch out onto the street outside this small dining room. Chef Caude Troisgros, the man behind Rio's Michelin-starred Olympe restaurant (*see page 35*), established T T Burger in 2014 with the aim of elevating the simple beef burger through high-quality Brazilian produce. He now has outlets in Barra da Tijuca and Leblon too.

The menu is not extensive – diners can choose between a single or double beef patty – but the burgers are a treat, made from fine cuts of Brazilian meat and topped with homemade family-recipe guava ketchup. Don't miss the Nutella shake either. You'll know when your meal is ready: the kitchen staff shout out your name through a little yellow megaphone when it's time to collect.
Rua Francisco Otaviano, 67
+ 55 (21) 2227 1192
troisgrosbrasil.com.br

⑩
Lasai, Botafogo
Top-of-the-line dining

When Lasai opened in 2014 in an old house in Botafogo it immediately set the standard for Brazilian haute cuisine. Chef and owner Rafael Costa e Silva studied in New York before moving to Spain to work with chef Andoni Luis Aduriz at the two-Michelin-starred Mugaritz in San Sebastian.

Lasai has two set menus a day: one giving diners a choice of ingredients, the other a "surprise" menu directed entirely by the chef. Both depend on what the earth and ocean can offer on a given day, with ingredients sourced from friends, local producers and the restaurant's two gardens.

We recommend putting your dining experience into Costa e Silva's hands; sommelier Oliver González and house barman Rodolfo Werner are also both stars in their own right. Lasai earned its first Michelin star in 2015.
Rua Conde de Irajá, 191
+ 55 (21) 3449 1834
lasai.com.br

Many hands

While Rio isn't known for service, that's not for want of manpower. Most good restaurants have an ecosystem of staff, from valets and doormen to waiters and bus boys. Tipping each is not usual (aside from your valet); a 10 per cent service fee is often included in your bill.

Mmmm, that água de coco looks good – let me taste

Must-try
Vatapá from Espírito Santa, Santa Teresa

Vatapá is a creamy concoction of bread, coconut cream, prawns and a variety of nuts. If you can't try it in the northeastern state of Bahia where it is a staple then, by golly, head to this charming Santa Teresa restaurant. Prepared by two cheery cooks, the *vatapá* here is first class; the establishment also has an impressive selection of cachaça.

espiritosanta.com.br

Know your dishes

Farofa: toasted manioc flour spiced with onions and herbs.
Pão de queijo: cheese bread.
Feijoada: stew of black beans, pork and salted beef.
Picanha: cap of rump typically barbecued over charcoal.
Picadinho: stew of filet mignon served with rice, farofa, banana and an egg.

⑪ Comuna, Botafogo
Entertainment all-rounder

Botafogo, nestled in between Copacabana, Jardim Botânico and Flamengo Beach, is one of Rio's real up-and-coming neighbourhoods; a place to find great bars and restaurants as well as a bit of an alternative scene.

Comuna exemplifies what makes the neighbourhood so attractive. It's predominantly a restaurant but the building (which was once a music studio) also houses an event and gallery space and an independent book publisher. The venture was started by four friends from Rio in 2011 to host music performances and exhibitions but it was transformed into a conventional restaurant in 2013. Today it's a popular hangout for the younger residents of Botafogo, who hold the burgers and milkshakes in particularly high regard.
Rua Sorocaba, 585
+ 55 (21) 3029 0789
comuna.cc

⑫ Esplanada Grill, Ipanema
Cut above

Hidden behind large tinted windows, Esplanada Grill is discreet yet buzzing on the inside. The wooden dining room can seat up to 65 and most tables have a view out onto the Ipanema street life. While it's an ideal spot for a business lunch, it's also a popular place for family lunches on the weekend.

The restaurant's success owes as much to the top-notch Argentinian and Uruguayan meats as to the man behind the grill, Luis José da Silva. Expect grilled meat and fish with side dishes to share – try the cashew-fruit caipirinha while you wait.
Rua Barão da Torre, 600
+ 55 (21) 2512 2970
esplanadagrill.com.br

⑬ Sushi Shin Miura, Centro
Hidden gem

To say that you would never stumble across Sushi Shin Miura is a huge understatement: the restaurant is in a nondescript electronics mall. The setting is nothing special but it's worth it to experience some of the best sushi in the city.

The *combinado* sushi selections are all excellent, as is the crispy pork katsu. The service, orchestrated by owner João Lima, is exceptional too. Ordinarily we might suggest avoiding the lunchtime rush but when this place is rammed with businessmen in suits it adds to the atmosphere.
Shopping Avenida Central,
Avenida Rio Branco, 156
+ 55 (21) 2262 3043
shinmiura.com.br

01 Uniko, Centro:
This sophisticated and
reliable Italian restaurant is
in the Sul América Arcade:
a 1920s construction
designed by French
architect Joseph Gire,
who was also behind the
Belmond Copacabana
Palace. Perfect for a light
business lunch.
unikorestaurante.com.br

02 Guimas, Baixo Gávea:
This 1980s establishment
is a traditional hangout for
Rio's bohemian crowd.
Both casual and refined,
Guimas is a collision
between a French bistro
and Carioca *boteco*.
Try to bag a table on the
open-air veranda.
restauranteguimas.com.br

03 Roberta Sudbrack,
Jardim Botânico
After several years
cooking at the country's
presidential palace,
Roberta Sudbrack
opened her eponymous
restaurant in Rio's Jardim
Botânico district. The
set menus carry a strong
Brazilian identity through
experimentation with
local ingredients.
robertasudbrack.com.br

04 Satyricon, Ipanema
This place has been
dubbed the best in town
for seafood. Whether
you want fresh scampi,
lobsters and oysters
from Rio, king crabs from
Alaska or salmon from
Norway this is the spot.
satyricon.com.br

05 Volta, Jardim Botânico
This contemporary
restaurant is based in an
old mansion restored by
famous architect Chicô
Gouvea. The food plays
on traditional recipes with
a modern twist.
restaurantevolta.com.br

⑭
Aconchego Carioca, Praça da
Bandeira
Comforting Brazilian food

Lacking the picturesque charm of
Rio's Zona Sul, the area of Praça da
Bandeira – close to the Maracanã
Stadium – has previously not been
a drawcard for visitors. But now the
area is being revitalised and amid
the new developments that are
sprouting up is the unpretentious
and charming Aconchego Carioca
(the name means "Carioca
comfort" in Portuguese).

This relaxed pub-style
restaurant sports a colourful interior
and serves food that is typical of
Brazil's northeast. If you need a
break from Rio's carnivorous
leanings this is a good option: the
restaurant has some great vegetarian
interpretations of classic dishes too.
Try the plantain and heart-of-palm
muqueca. Another highlight of the
house is its excellent beer selection,
which is one of the most extensive
in the city.
Barão de Iguatemi, 379
+55 (21) 2273 9035

15
Aprazivel, Santa Teresa
Green dining

With its treehouse-like structure where you can lunch in a straw-ceilinged hut with views out over Guanabara Bay, Aprazivel has an elegant tropical feel.

The establishment started when founder and chef Ana Castilho opened her house as accommodation for visitors to the first Arte de Portas Abertas cultural weekend back in 1997. The place has been running ever since with the help of Ana's two sons João and Pedro Hermeto.

The menu features Brazilian house classics with ingredients sourced from the Amazon and small nearby producers. Try the Carioca rice made with prawns, coconut and ginger. The restaurant also brews its own beer, the perfect refreshment after a walk in the nearby hills.
Rua Aprazivel, 62
+55 (21) 2508 9174
aprazivel.com.br

Table vista
Aprazível has spectacular views over Rio

(16)
Olympe, Lagoa
Food from the gods

Run by French chef Claude
Troisgros and his son Thomas,
Olympe is one of Rio's best high-
end restaurants. Claude moved
to Brazil in 1979 and set up the
restaurant in 1983, combining
French culinary techniques with
Brazilian ingredients such as heart
of palm and yucca flour.
   "The cuisine is French, which
basically means we use a lot of
butter and a lot of cream," says
Thomas. "But there's always
a Brazilian twist. It's very
contemporary, not classically
French at all."
Rua Custódio Serrão, 62
+ 55 (21) 2539 4542
olympe.com.br

Must-try
Feijoada from Bar do Bonde,
Santa Teresa
Come the weekend this off-
the-beaten-track *boteco* hums
with live samba and diners
clamouring for its trademark
dish. *Feijoada* is considered
Brazil's national food and in its
proper incarnation it's a lusty
black-bean stew that's slow
cooked with pork off-cuts,
beef and various sausages. Its
ingredients reflect Brazil's rich
ethnic make-up and here it's
served with rice and sautéed
kale, topped with toasted
farofa (*see box, page 32*).
cargocollective.com/
bardobonde

(17)
Baalbek, Copacabana
Religious experience

A small portrait of Saint Charbel
– the 19th-century monk revered
by Lebanon's Maronite Christian
community – keeps a careful eye
from behind the cash register at this
popular Lebanese snack spot as the
stream of customers ebbs and flows.
Founded in 1959 by José Chaachaa,
who emigrated to Rio from Zahle
in Lebanon, this simple foodstop is
now run by his daughter Miriam.
Her cooks prepare the Levantine
delicacies at 05.30 each morning,
from *kibbeh* meat patties to
glistening, sticky baklava.
Galeria Menescal,
Avenida Nossa Senhora
de Copacabana, 664
+ 55 (21) 2255 4574

(18)
Bar do Mineiro, Santa Teresa
Stew sensation

The owners, staff and food at
this unpretentious yet graceful
establishment come from the nearby
state of Minas Gerais, which is known
for its cuisine throughout the country.
Diógenes Paixão opened
Bar do Mineiro back in 1992 and has
been catering for Rio's artistic and
bohemian types ever since.

People flock in for its famous
feijoada (see box, page 32) which was
a favourite of renowned landscape
artist Roberto Burle Marx. Make
sure you turn your eye to the
interesting decor on its walls curated
by Paixão himself, an avid art buff.
Rua Paschoal Carlos Magno, 99
+55 (21) 2221 9227
bardomineiro.net

(19)
Rubaiyat, Jardim Botânico
All fired up

This is the first Rio branch of the
successful chain that has since
spread across South and Central
America – it's even landed in
Madrid. The menu revolves around
sumptuous cuts of beef, mostly
from cattle reared on Rubaiyat's
own ranch in Mato Grosso do Sul
in western Brazil.

The meat is grilled and
served with typical Brazilian
accompaniments. Although the
food is excellent, the main draw is
the setting: windows overlook Rio's
horseracing track, which is itself a
treasure in the heart of the city.
Rua Jardim Botânico, 971
+55 (21) 3204 9999
rubaiyat.com.br

Nose to tail
—
The chair
leather also
comes from
the ranch

At the beach

People often underestimate
the significance of beach
commerce in Rio. The sellers
who roam across the sands,
peddling everything from
food and drinks to beach
towels, bikinis and sunscreen,
generate billions of reais a
year. When it comes to food,
here are some of the must-try
seaside snacks they tout.

01 Globo biscuits: These
    air-puffed doughnuts
    made from manioc flour
    are the perfect snack to
    stave off hunger before
    lunch. They come in two
    flavours: savoury in green
    wrapping and sweet in
    red. These biscuits are
    so integral to a day at
    the beach that vendors
    have been designated
    as intangible cultural
    heritage by city hall.
02 Corn on the cob: This
    healthy snack comes
    rolled in its leaves and
    you can smell it from
    miles away.
03 Picolé (ice lolly) Itália:
    Itália ice lollies are a
    cooling treat. But when in
    Rio, forget the chocolate
    and vanilla flavours – why
    not venture towards
    the mango, coconut or
    passion-fruit varieties?
04 Matte Leão: This iced-tea
    beverage is made from
    dried yerba mate leaves;
    the usage of the herb
    goes way back to Brazil's
    native Guaraní tribe. The
    bitter-sweet refreshment
    is sold on the beach by
    chanting vendors carrying
    two metal gallons; one
    of *mate* and one of
    lemonade, which you
    can mix to your liking.

⑳ Chico e Alaíde, Leblon
Labour of love

This classic *boteco* is situated on the corner of Rua Dias Ferreira, one of Rio's leafiest and most salubrious retail streets, and the louder and busier Avenida Bartolomeu Mitre.

The two founders, Francisco "Chico" das Chagas Gomes Filho and Alaíde Carneiro, met while they were working as a barman and a cook respectively at another *boteco* around the corner: the iconic Bracarense. They dreamed of setting up on their own and did so in 2008.

The menu features 45 different types of finger food. Our pick is the *choquinho*, a prawn and cheese-curd mix wrapped in crispy, deep-fried potato noodles.

"We're trying to compete with the *botecos* that have been here 20 or 30 years," says Chico. "People always tell me 'Chico, you're like an elephant – you were born big.'"
Rua Dias Ferreira, 679
+ 55 (21) 2512 0028
chicoealaide.com.br

I'm bringing wine culture to Rio one glass at a time

㉑ Rancho Português, Ipanema
Portuguese dining with feeling

Brazil is home to several Portuguese restaurants but Rancho Português is the place to go for an authentic experience. The journey begins from the moment you step into the wood-panelled interior *(pictured above)* and hear the melancholic strains of *fado*.

The menu is rich with fish delicacies, including 13 different cod interpretations. Don't miss the octopus with olive oil and garlic and leave room for custard tarts and *rabanadas* (the Portuguese version of French toast) for dessert. And a glass of port too, of course.
Rua Maria Quitéria, 136
+ 55 (21) 2287 0335
ranchoportuguesrio.com.br

㉒ Nova Capela, Lapa
Heritage experience

This classic bar and restaurant opened in 1923 at another location; it's been in its current spot in the 300-year-old neighbourhood of Lapa since 1967. In 2011, Nova Capela was awarded Cultural Heritage Site status.

The well-mannered and snappily dressed waiters evoke old-school tradition; this is an established favourite rather than a trendy hotspot. It attracts an eclectic bohemian mix of musicians, writers and intellectuals until the kitchen stops serving at about 05.00.

Keep away from the tourist crowds during daytime and opt for dinner instead; the vibe here changes completely as day turns to night. We strongly recommend booking a table with a group of friends and ordering the cod fishcakes along with wild boar and roasted goat.
Avenida Mem de Sá, 96
+ 55 (21) 2252 6228

Must-try
Fish of the day at Eça, Centro

Eça is – in many ways – a hidden gem. It's actually in the basement of a luxury jewellery shop, H Stern, in Rio's corporate heart. It's a popular place for business lunches and this is one of the few spots where you'll see the majority of men wearing suits (no ties though, naturally).

Belgian chef Frédéric de Maeyer came to Rio when he was 25 and dreamed of starting his own restaurant. "I fell in love with Brazil and with the people," he says. "I met Claude Troisgros (see page 31) and he said there was a real opportunity to grow here." In 2001, Maeyer returned to Rio and founded Eça. The grilled fish of the day is our pick; it is served with plantain and rocket pesto.
hstern.com.br

Albamar, Centro
Old-time favourite

When the grand 19th-century wrought-iron-and-glass tower that houses this seafood restaurant was threatened with demolition in the 1960s (to make way for a viaduct), residents from across Rio raised their voices to have it saved (former US vice-president Nelson Rockerfeller also flew in to sign the petition).

Chef Luiz Walter Incao, who spent much of his career in kitchens across Australia, pairs Brazilian classics such as *pirão* fish broth with wines from Chile, Argentina and Portugal, and sparkling wine from southern Brazil.
Praça Marechal Âncora, 184
+ 55 (21) 2240 8378
albamar.com.br

Majórica, Flamengo
For the grill of it

Rio's cuisine is dominated by meat – and lots of it. *Churrascarias* are restaurants that serve all-you-can-eat meat barbecued on an open fire. It is brought to your table on skewers, where waiters slice it onto plates. While these restaurants were once popular with Cariocas, they have slightly fallen out of fashion in recent years. Majórica is the exception.

Step through an unassuming door into the cavernous wood-panelled room dominated by a huge grill. Instead of paying a fixed price for all the meat you could possibly want, at Majórica you select the cut of beef.
Rua Senador Vergueiro, 11/15
+ 55 (21) 2205 6820
majoricario.com.br

Celeiro, Leblon
Salad days

A favoured spot for Leblon's ladies who lunch, Celeiro was one of the first restaurants in Rio to offer self-serve dining when it opened its doors in 1982. "I think we started the movement!" says Lucia Lacombe Hertz, who manages the restaurant with her sister Beatriz.

Their mother, Maria Rosa, arrives at 07.00 each morning to begin the day's cooking. The menu includes salads of potatoes, fish and seasonal vegetables sourced from nearby, as well as sweet treats including chocolate-and-avocado mousse and homemade truffles.
Rua Dias Ferreira, 199
+ 55 (21) 2274 7843
celeiroculinaria.com.br

Drinks
Getting into the spirit

③
Casa Momus, Lapa
Drink in the history

Every corner of Casa Momus has a story, from the wooden "library" shelves behind the bar appropriated from a treasured wine shop upon its closure to the pen-and-ink illustrations on the walls by celebrated Brazilian artist and children's TV personality Daniel Azulay. Upstairs there's an attractive dining table by famous Brazilian designer Sérgio Rodrigues.

After a plate from the Italian-inspired menu and a cocktail or two, why not while away your evening at the fabled Rio Scenarium dance hall just across the street?
Rue do Lavradio, 11
+55 (21) 3852 8250
casamomus.com.br

①
Academia da Cachaça, Leblon
Caipirinha craftsmanship

Brazil's national drink, the caipirinha, is not complicated – at its simplest it's a blend of ice, sugar, lime and the sugar-cane spirit cachaça – but it can be done well and not so well.

At this bar in the heart of Leblon there are more than 100 types of cachaça to choose from and the bar staff, some of whom have worked here for 30 years, are experts. It does get busy at weekends, serving about 400 caipirinhas a day, so be prepared for a bit of a scrum. There's also excellent food – the *feijoada* (*see box, page 32*) and the *escondidinho* (jerked beef served with cheese) are famous.
Rua Conde de Bernadotte, 26
+55 (21) 2239 1542
academiadacachaca.com.br

②
Astor, Ipanema
Breezy beach brews

This may be an offshoot of a São Paulo bar but its unparalleled location in Rio, looking out on Ipanema Beach, gives it the edge. The interiors are reminiscent of an art deco Paris brasserie with wood tables, mirrored surfaces and tiled floors but there is also a large veranda out front for those who prefer a sea breeze.

The house trademark is the beer – served with a three-finger-high foam head – but Astor also prides itself on its spirits selection and skilled barmen. Don't miss the saffron rice balls and shrimp *empadinha* (mini pies).
Avenida Vieira Souto, 110
+55 (21) 2523 0085
barastor.com.br

Raising a glass
—
On Casa Momus's cocktail list you'll spot Madame Satã (Madame Satan), which commemorates one of Rio's most famous drag acts. Born into poverty in 1900, Madame Satã (real name João Francisco dos Santos) became a symbol of the struggle of the poor in Rio.

Juice bars

Making a stop at a juice bar is a daily ritual for many Cariocas. Most don't have tables or seating: you order across the counter and often eat and drink at it too.

When ordering a juice (*suco* in Portuguese) simply choose the combination of fruits you want and the juice-maker will do the rest. It's a good opportunity to sample some lesser-known Amazonian fruits such as the lychee-like *graviola*, the bitter orange *acerola* fruit or the gloopy, purple açaí which some say tastes like a mix of berries and chocolate (many Cariocas combine it with granola for a nutritious breakfast).

Many juice bars are also open until late and become a hangout after a night out on the tiles.

01 BB Lanches
Rua Aristídes Espínola, 64
02 Bibi Sucos
Rua Maria Quitéria, 70
03 Natural e Sabor
Rua Visconde de Pirajá, 611

④
Bar Sobe, Jardim Botânico
The only way is up

A discreet stairway in an old mansion leads to the rooftop and Bar Sobe. On Saturday afternoons there's a barbecue for tasty burgers, while on Wednesdays and Sundays DJs spin disco and pop records for a lively crowd of up to 100.

The menu is filled with playful reinterpretations of classic cocktails and there are delicious nibbles. But the real charm of the place lies undoubtedly in its knockout views of Christ the Redeemer and the Imperial Palm trees of Jardim Botânico.
Rua Pacheco Leão, 732
+55 (21) 3114 7691

⑥
Palaphita Kitch, Lagoa
City escape

Before Janaina Milward and her husband Mario Andrade opened Palaphita Kitch in 2004 this stretch of lagoon was devoid of life. "It used to be a drab, forgotten place," says Milward. Named and modelled after the waterside dwellings of northern Brazil, the bar is now a tranquil spot for soaking up a sunset.

Try a signature cocktail: a caipirinha made with either the juice of the small, black *jabuticaba* berry or the sweet, orange *siriguela* fruit. "We created this magical place and it's right in the middle of a big city," says Milward.
Avenida Epitácio Pessoa, Kiosk 20
+55 (21) 2227 0837
palaphitakitch.com.br

⑤
Baixo Gávea
Party like a local

Pinched between The Jockey Club, Leblon and Jardim Botânico, Baixo Gávea (known as "BG") is a place to drink, spill out onto the street, meet people and repeat until you have hit all the bars on the block. A popular gathering spot for artists and students, Baixo Gávea is Carioca informality exemplified.

The most lively nights are Thursdays and Sundays. From 22.00 on it becomes a boisterous concentration of 18- to 40-year-olds. You can order food and drinks to consume on the pavement – try the *picanha (see box, page 32)* from Braseiro da Gávea – or you can eat inside one of the many bars if you get in early enough.

I hear Complex Esquina is the place to meet pretty birds

(7)
Complex Esquina 111, Ipanema
Creative entertainment hub

This mixed-use development towards the back streets of Ipanema is a cultural space, restaurant and bar all in one. It's the creative brainchild of three entertainment-production companies. The mezzanine hosts exhibitions during the day and converts to a loud and upscale bar at night.

DJ Zeh Pretim, a well-known figure on Rio's night scene and one of the partners at Complex Esquina, ensures toes are kept tapping with a mix of old-school funk and soul.
Rua Maria Quitéria, 111
+ 55 (21) 3256 9375
thecomplex.com.br

(8)
Bar dos Descasados, Santa Teresa
Sunset romance

When the building that now houses the Santa Teresa Hotel was a colonial farmhouse, the slave quarters were under the arches in the basement. This is now where the hotel's bar can be found. It has kept its nickname – which means "bar for unmarried people" – from its other previous incarnation as a slightly down-at-heel, cheap-and-cheerful hotel before the current owners took over in 2008 and gave it a glamorous new look.

The floor tiles and the walls are original while the art on the walls comes from the studios of Santa Teresa artists such as Atelier Zemog. It's another wonderful spot for a sundowner or two; the large arches open out onto one of the best views in Rio, over the rooftops of Santa Teresa to Guanabara Bay.
Rua Almirante Alexandrino, 660
+ 55 (21) 2222 2755
santa-teresa-hotel.com

Jammin'
—
Order a fresh fruit cocktail to share

Local flavour
Botecos

Rio icon
—
Bracarense
in Leblon is
a legendary
'boteco'

The small bars known as *botecos* aren't unique to Rio – they were introduced by the Portuguese settlers so are found across Brazil – but they have taken on a greater cultural significance here. Part of that is down to the weather and the easygoing Carioca attitude. These simple venues serving *chope* (draught beer) and finger food are almost always open to the elements, so on evenings and weekends the crowds often commandeer the pavement outside to enjoy the last few hours of sun.

Botecos, or *botequins* (the names are interchangeable), are ideal pit-stops at the end of a busy workday or an afternoon at the beach. Cariocas will debate fiercely which are the best in Rio, and even what the judging criteria should be. But in general a good *boteco* will serve ice-cold *chope* in a clean glass – with not too much of a *colarinho* (frothy top) – as well as great bar snacks, and will have plenty of space outside to spill out onto.

The selection is basically the same everywhere: small pies filled with either prawn or crab, *bolinhos do bacalhau* (cod balls) and *pastéis* (pastry parcels filled with either cheese or meat). Although simple, not every *boteco* gets these right – and Cariocas know very well which places do.

More botecos to frequent

01 Jobi, Leblon:
Probably Rio's most famous *boteco*. It was opened in 1956 and continues to draw a mixed, rowdy crowd, especially on Friday and Saturday nights.
jobibar.com.br

02 Pavão Azul, Copacabana:
A Copacabana classic, this bustling bar serves relaxed a range of Brazilian snacks and has plenty of seats out on the street.
+55 (21) 2236 2381

03 Bar Urca, Urca:
This bar in the sleepy Urca neighbourhood is a great stopping-off point after work; it also has some of the best crab pies in town. Grab a beer and sit on the seawall with the locals to watch the sun go down over the bay.
barurca.com.br

04 Bracarense, Leblon:
Another of Rio's post-beach institutions, Bracarense is popular with the trendy Leblon crowd. The terrace is packed every weekend.
bracarense.com.br

05 Bar do Gomes, Santa Teresa:
This old-school haunt can be found among the grand, slightly crumbling houses of Rua Aurea. It's not the type of place you would simply stumble across – and as such, it's mainly frequented by loyal denizens of Santa Teresa.
+55 (21) 2232 0822

Beach business
—— Sunrise industry

Every morning in Rio an army of entrepreneurial vendors takes over the city's tens of kilometres of beach and turns them into a tropical bazaar of sorts. There are the drink-sellers with casks strapped over their shoulders, one for sweet lemonade, the other for Matte Leão iced tea. Then there are the men holding enormous bags full of crispy, light-as-air Globo biscuits (*see page 36*) and the canga vendors with dozens of brightly coloured beach towels.

Each vendor calls out to the sun-worshippers on the sand and many have a distinctive yell that locals instantly recognise. Some sing witty rhymes; others wear eye-catching costumes. But this is not simply theatre: it's big business. By some estimates, Rio's beach commerce makes about R$7bn a year for the city. That's quite a few pineapple slices and caipirinhas.

Retail
— Laidback design with flair

Fashion in Rio is relatively simple. The Carioca style is low-key and most people head straight from the beach to restaurants and bars; a collared shirt will often set you apart from the crowd. The shops across the city reflect this preference, offering mostly beachwear and casual daywear. More formal options are inevitably less well evolved. It should also be said that there are more shops for women than men, perhaps because Rio women tend to make more of an effort than their male counterparts.

Nonetheless there are a host of thriving homegrown brands making clothes in Brazil and selling domestically. This is largely down to the fact that importing clothes is prohibitively bureaucratic and expensive in Brazil – the success of local brands is a great upshot.

You'll find most of the best retail around Ipanema and Leblon but Lapa and Jardim Botânico are also great locations to find furniture and homeware.

Menswear
Made for the beach

Going global
Osklen is taking Rio style to the world

① Osklen, Ipanema
Beach plus

Although Oskar Metsavaht's beach- and sportswear brand Osklen is now global – with shops from Tokyo to Miami – its origins are in the fishing village of Búzios, a weekend getaway for Rio's upper crust. It was founded in 1989 and the first Rio store opened two years later. The brand straddles taste: Osklen Collection offers high-end casualwear while Osklen Praia is a range of T-shirts and shorts. You can find both within 200 metres of each other in Ipanema.
*Rua Maria Quitéria, 85 (flagship),
+55 (21) 2227 2911;
Rua Prudente de Morais, 1102
(Osklen Praia)
+55 (21) 2522 3641
osklen.com*

Shopping malls

While taking a stroll inside the walls of a big mall isn't to everyone's taste (especially considering Rio's enviable climate), should a rainy day interrupt your trip these are our top picks for Rio's indoor shopping destinations.

01 Village Mall, Barra da Tijuca: The air-conditioned walkways of this luxury-retail behemoth have everything from Louis Vuitton, Armani and Cartier to the city's only Apple store. You can also find a cinema, theatre and high-end dining spots. *shoppingvillagemall.com.br*

02 Fashion Mall, São Conrado: The retail and dining selection is luxurious and this mall has a quiet, exclusive feel. *fashionmall.com.br*

03 Rio Design Leblon, Leblon: This small mall in the middle of Leblon has more of a neighbourhood feel and is less imposing than others. When here pick up a *brigadeiro* (chocolate sweet) at the Fabiana D'Angelo kiosk. *riodesignleblon.com.br*

② Reserva, Ipanema
Carioca casual

In 2004, Rio-based entrepreneurs Rony Meisler (*pictured*) and Fernando Sigal asked themselves a question: why was it that in a beach-loving city such as Rio, Osklen (*see opposite*) was the only player in the men's beach-shorts market? So to the drawing board they went – and the designs flew off the shelves.

Now offering casual clothing for men, from contemporary button-down shirts to colourful chinos, Reserva boasts 38 shops across the country, with sister stores for women (Eva) and children (Mini) too.
Rua Maria Quitéria, 77
+55 (21) 2247 5980
usereserva.com

I hope they let dogs on the tram

3

Alberto Gentleman, Ipanema
Formal outfitter

This stalwart on the Brazilian fashion scene has been dressing the men of Rio for more than 70 years. Inspired by the tailoring of London's Savile Row, the company runs its own workroom to produce ranges of formal, casual and sportswear. The team of 50 tailors uses the finest Italian, French and English fabrics and also offers bespoke services. For a higher fee, an Alberto Gentleman tailor can bring the fitting session to you and have your customised shoes, suit and shirt ready within 15 working days.
Rua Visconde de Pirajá, 282
+55 (21) 2522 6925
albertogentleman.com

4

Foxton, Ipanema
Call of the ocean

Foxton is the new kid on the block. The brand was set up by Rodrigo Ribeiro and Marcella Mendes in 2008; they now have six shops around the city. While the aesthetic is still casual and designed to suit the beach, the couple have focused on high-quality production. For Ribeiro it's about advancing fashion while staying true to Rio's attitude: "In São Paulo, you see the same clothes as in Paris and New York. We don't want to make copies; we want to bring trends from around the world and translate them for Rio. Foxton is a very Rio brand."
Rua Garcia d'Ávila, 147
+55 (21) 3202 2692
foxtonbrasil.com.br

5

Richards, Ipanema
Nautical lines

In a city known for its beach lifestyle, Richards has cornered the market in smart menswear staples. While the brand has numerous shops around the city, this stand-alone space in Ipanema is the one to go for. There is also homeware alongside clothing for women and kids.
Rua Maria Quitéria, 95
+55 (21) 2522 1245
richards.com.br

 6

Blue Man, Ipanema
In-demand swimwear

Brothers David and Simão Azulay made Blue Man into a success story during the 1970s by adding their vibrant prints to pieces such as the tie-side bikini and *sungas*: the swimming shorts favoured by fashionable men throughout Brazil. Keeping things in family, David's daughter Sharon assumed the role of creative director in 2009.
  Head here for sportswear and swimming costumes for the whole family. There are nine Blue Man shops in Rio alone but, for its proximity to the beach, we favour the Ipanema branch.
Rua Visconde de Pirajá, 351
+55 (21) 2247 4905
blueman.com.br

Outdoor markets

Rio is home to many outdoor markets selling everything from antiques to vintage clothes, stationery to Carnival costumes. Just remember to bring your best bargaining skills. Here are our favourites.

01 Feira de São Cristóvão, São Cristóvão: This market is a purpose-built arena hosting almost 700 stalls of traditional crafts and food, music and entertainment from Brazil's northeast. Open Tuesday to Sunday.

02 Feira de Antiguidades da Praça XV, Centro: Visiting this antiques market is like stepping back in time: you'll find typewriters, badges, stamps and old books. Open Saturday.

03 Feira do Rio Antigo, Lapa: Held on the first Saturday of the month, this lively market on Rua do Lavradio sells everything from antiques and handicrafts to clothing and records, all to the strains of samba.

04 Praça Santos Dumont antique market, Baixo Gávea: Every Sunday, stalls are set up selling antiques of all kinds. Expect books, ceramics, paintings, carpets and bric-a-brac.

05 Saara, Centro: If you can't find what you're looking for in Saara you probably won't find it anywhere in the whole of Rio. With 70,000 shoppers a day, this is the place for a bargain. Established by immigrants from Syria, Lebanon, Greece, Turkey, China, South Korea and Japan, the buzzing market is ideal if you're looking for a Carnival costume.

Womenswear
Beyond palm-tree prints

1

Cris Barros, Leblon
Standout soft shades

Cris Barros's womenswear is chic and low-key. Expect neutral colours (a rarity in Rio) and easy-care materials. There is also a strong selection of elegant party dresses. The company is a native of São Paulo but since opening in 2002 it has expanded to six locations throughout Brazil, including two in Rio de Janeiro.
Rio Design Mall, Avenida Ataulfo de Paiva, 270
+55 (21) 2512 5072
crisbarros.com.br

2

Jenessequá, Leblon
Sport smart

Anna Luiza Padua, one of Jenessequá's founders (alongside Jacqueline Cabral and Bia Brasil), was in a restaurant when she spotted a problem with a group of women nearby. "They were trying to look nice but they were wearing gym clothes," she says. She pondered why activewear meant having to forego sartorial style. Jenessequá, which opened in 2013, produces "comfortable chic", says Cabral. Soft, loose blouses and simple wrap-dresses, all designed and made in Rio, are staples.
Rua Dias Ferreira, 64
Sala 307
+55 (21) 3251 8839
jenessequa.com.br

3

Adriana Degreas, Barra da Tijuca
Beach beautiful

Founded in 2001 by Brazilian swimwear designer Adriana Degreas, this brand is the go-to when it comes to luxury beachwear in Rio. The slick boutique, which opened in the Village Mall in 2012, is the work of interior designers Nórea de Vitto and Beto Galvez. Even though Degreas is from São Paulo, she has a deep connection with Rio. "My first big show was at the Copacabana Palace," she says. Her classy swimwear and clothing designs avoid all the clichés; there's not a palm-tree print to be found.
Village Mall, Avenida das Américas, 3900
+55 (21) 3252 2562
adrianadegreas.com.br

Costume change

If you're female and find yourself on the beach without a bikini you don't have to go topless. Swimwear vendors roam the sands; they tie their wares to the spokes of umbrellas. A two-piece set should cost no more than R$100; single pieces can be bought for R$30.

④
Maria Manuela, Leblon
Climate control

Although it's tucked away in a narrow building in Rua Dias Ferreira, this small womenswear shop is worth seeking out. Designer Manuela Noronha started out selling elegant and comfortable white shirts. "I have always been involved with fashion: my mother owned a garment manufacturer," she says. "I made my own dolls' clothes. She also worked for a stint with Brazilian bikini designer Lenny Niemeyer. She now creates fluid dresses and skirts using light knitwear, lace and crochet, which are all materials suited to the warm Rio climate.
Rua Dias Ferreira, 417
+ 55 (21) 2511 4845
mariamanuela.net

Vix Paula Hermanny, Leblon
Jumpsuits for joy

Vix is named after the Brazilian island of Vitória where founder Paula Hermanny grew up. Its first flagship store opened in Rio in 2013. The brand is famous for its swimwear but also creates dresses and jumpsuits, plus accessories.
Rio Design Leblon, Avenida Ataulfo de Paiva, 270
+ 55 (21) 2279 4749
vixpaulahermanny.com

Rio rocks

Antonio Bernardo is a Rio-born jeweller who founded his eponymous brand in 1981. His masterful team of goldsmiths handcrafts the collection which is often embellished with high-grade stones. There are six outposts across the city including the Ipanema flagship.

⑥
Virzi + De Luca, Leblon
Shining example

Founded in 2012 by established womenswear designer Marcella Virzi and fashion icon Betina de Luca (a sort of Carioca Alexa Chung), this jewellery brand produces sculptural and playful pieces. Inspired by the surrealism movement, the designs are spirited and free – just like the essence of Rio de Janeiro. Expect to find chunky neck pieces influenced by ancient Egyptian styles, rings and beaded bracelets, plus pineapple- and crustacean-emblazoned necklaces and earrings.
Rua Dias Ferreira, 175
Sala 405
+ 55 (21) 982 331 243
virzideluca.com

Bikini, check. Flip-flops, check. I'm Rio-ready

Salinas, Leblon
Brazilian institution

Jacqueline and Tunico De Biase founded this well-known Brazilian swimwear brand in Salinas in the state of Minas Gerais in 1982. Irreverence is part of its DNA. "I grew up going to Ipanema Beach and the young people from my generation in the 1970s often created their own bikinis to escape from the more traditional models," says Jacqueline. "That's how Salinas began, right here in the sands of Rio de Janeiro."

Madonna and Naomi Campbell have been seen in Salinas designs. The fun, colourful swimwear is displayed alongside summery jewellery and other beachy must-haves such as flip-flops, towels, and totes. The brand now has 42 shops around Brazil (two opened in November 2015) and is sold in 25 other countries, including the US, France and Japan.
Rio Design, Avenida Ataulfo de Paiva, 270
+ 55 (21) 2512 9734
salinascompras.com.br

Green team
——
Farm has grown into a success story

⑧
Farm, Ipanema
Hippy exotica

Kátia Barros and Marcello Bastos have come a long way since starting Farm as a stand in the Babilônia Feira Hype open-air market in the 1990s. Since their first Copacabana store, the womenswear brand has grown into a fashion emporium with more than 60 outlets throughout Brazil and a lovely children's brand called A Fábula. The style is distinctly jovial with lots of vibrant prints. You'll find plenty of tropical patterns on dresses, shirts, bags and shoes and interesting collaborations with brands such as Havaianas and Adidas.
Rua Visconde de Pirajá, 365
+55 (21) 3813 3817
farmrio.com.br

⑨
Felipa, Leblon
Espadrille heaven

Felipa owner Mariana Luchi (*pictured*) says that she "chose to be happy" when in 2010 she quit her career in finance to begin designing her own range of espadrilles, inspired by those she'd seen while on holiday in Rome. Opened in 2012, this small colourful store in Leblon, designed by Rio-based architect Miguel Pinto Guimarães, boasts an ingenious floor-to-ceiling storage system of wall-mounted chairs and stools. It attracts women of all ages in search of espadrilles to add a twist to eveningwear or a playful look for a day on the beach.
Rua Dias Ferreira, 116A
+55 (21) 3114 6408
felipa.com.br

⑩
Adriana Barra, Leblon
Party pieces

The swirling patterns of womenswear designer Adriana Barra have become a recognisable feature of high-society soirées in Rio and beyond. This boutique is an intimate setting in which to try on pieces designed and made locally. Barra's inspiration derives from an array of sources – from Imperial Japan to Elvis Presley – and the price tags are as impressive as the clothes. The playful, patterned products from a recent collaboration with Brazil's Arno kitchenware manufacturer are also available to buy here.
Rua Dias Ferreira, 64
Sala 101
+55 (21) 2512 3320
adrianabarra.com.br

⑪
Lenny, Ipanema
Beachwear royalty

Renowned bikini-smith Lenny Niemeyer is often credited with being at the forefront of beach couture; take a look at the elegant cut of her swimwear and you'll understand why. Her Lenny brand has more than 20 boutiques around the country and can also be found in British, French and US retailers.
 Niemeyer's swimwear is a firm favourite with Rio's shiny, happy people; while the city may lag behind when it comes to conventional high-end fashion, its beach fashion is miles ahead and influences the world.
Rua Garcia D'Avila, 149
+55 (21) 2227 5537
lennyniemeyer.com

Concept stores
Unique takes

①
Q Guai, Ipanema
Anything goes

This is one of Rio's most novel concept stores. It was opened in 2004 by fashion designer Amanda Haegler in an attempt to soften the formality of women's retail. "It's rare to find lots of different things under one roof," says Haegler of her boutique, which now includes menswear, an art gallery and a coffee shop that local food producers take over for three months at a time. Among the new generation of Brazilian designers featured are the Lokalwear jewellery studio, T-shirts by Saint Matthias and trainers by Rio-based Odde.
Avenida Henrique Dumont, 65A
+55 (21) 2529 2263
qguai.com

Bright idea
—
Take a break
from shopping
in the onsite
café

Dona Coisa, Jardim Botânico
Exclusive fashion

This eclectic shop is on a street
that climbs through the Jardim
Botânico district. It opened in 2005
and quickly expanded into adjacent
houses, selling everything from
national and international clothing
brands to books and fragrances.

Don't expect too much colour
or print – the style is refined. Some
of the brands, such as Sonia Pinto's
chic womenswear, are exclusive.
There's also a fully equipped room
at the back that can be rented out
as a temporary workplace or for
business meetings.
Rua Lopes Quintas, 153
+55 (21) 2249 2336
donacoisa.com.br

Beauty spot
—
The first floor of Dona
Coisa is given over to a
shop-in-shop concept by
cosmetics brand Phebo.
There's also a charming café
that serves coffees, teas
and homemade cakes, and
sells a choice selection
of homeware.

③
Void General Store, Leblon
Street-art friendly

Void is a snappy concept boutique
where you'll find everything from
chewing gum to colourful beach
towels. The eclectic shops are
now found across Brazil. They
feature fridges stocked with juices
and beer, coffee bars and clothing
for both men and women, from
shorts to beach shoes. Racks of
spray paint for the city's street
artists (graffiti was legalised in
Rio in 2009) sit atop displays
of smart and playful notebooks
and paperbacks, including
a line of rather risqué colouring
books by Babel Books.
Ataulfo de Paiva, 1166
+55 (21) 3592 7719
avoid.com.br

This life's
supply of
Havaianas
will keep the
family happy

Home and interiors
With a dash of Rio zest

①
Poeira, Leblon
Modern Portuguese

Poeira ("dust") is the creation of
Portuguese entrepreneur Mónica
Penaguião; the homeware shops
hold a mix of international and
local designs. The branch on Rua
Dias Ferreira is home to pieces by
global brands including Cappellini,
Vitra and Flexform but it also stocks
"Made in Brazil" items, including
ceramics by Rosana Donate, textiles
by Adriana Barra (*see page 52*) and
pots and vases by Brunno Jahara.
Poeira also has own-brand furniture,
rugs and cushions.
Rua Dias Ferreira, 480
+55 (21) 2580 0513
poeiraonline.com

Novo Desenho

"Many visitors to the museum
ask if it is a permanent
exhibition," says Tulio Mariante
of his shop inside Museu de Arte
Do Rio. The carefully selected
collection of design items and
furniture includes pieces by the
likes of Sérgio Rodrigues, Lina
Bo Bardi, Ricardo Fasanello and
Zanini de Zanine.

② SK Mobília, Santo Cristo
Interiors treasure trove

SK Mobília has an unfussy yet robust offering of Brazilian and Portuguese design classics and an assortment of antique oddities, from the glass cabinets of Portugal's Joachim Deguerro to armchairs by Sérgio Rodrigues. Established 15 years ago, the store has moved from Centro to the former Fábrica Bhering chocolate factory (*see page 98*) in Santo Cristo. Founder Sérgio Menezes, armed with his encyclopaedic knowledge of design, also creates his own furniture – notably dining tables made from reclaimed wood.
Rua Orestes, 28
+55 (21) 2232 3451
skmobilia.com

③ Arquivo Contemporâneo, Ipanema
Local homeware classics

João Caetano and Ivo Wanderley's shop is the place to go for anyone after Brazilian homeware. The slick interiors were created by architect Alessandro Sartore with lighting by contemporary designer Maneco Quinderé.
　The collection encompasses modern furniture classics by icons such as Oscar Niemeyer and Jorge Zalszupin, as well as the work of contemporary greats such as Jader Almeida and Etel Carmona. Every season an architecture or design heavyweight is invited to reimagine the shop's display window.
Rua Redentor, 147
+55 (21) 2227 9121
arquivocontemporaneo.com.br

④ Mercado Moderno, Lapa
Past and present collide

The long exposed-brick gallery of Mercado Moderno is a fine companion to the numerous design shops along Lapa's picturesque Rua do Lavradio. A pared-back display of furniture stretching along its length includes pieces by established and emerging Brazilian designers; this is where to find sleek shelving units by Hugo Sigaud and fine examples of work from the late Italian-Brazilian modernist architect and designer Lina Bo Bardi. A team of friendly staff are on hand to walk you through the collection.
Rua do Lavradio, 130
+55 (21) 2508 6083
mercadomodernobrasil.com.br

6
Trousseau Maison, Ipanema
Sheets ahead

This luxury linen retailer has
come a long way since owners
Romeu and Adriana Trussardi
started selling imported bed linen
in São Paulo in the 1990s. Today
there are more than 20 shops in
Brazil and while the fabrics are
from Italy, the brand's collection
is manufactured on these shores.
   The Trussardis still run the
business, which now includes
homeware, babywear and
fragrances across six spaces in
the city. The luxurious interior of
the Ipanema location was designed
by Sandro Oberhammer.
Rua Garcia d'Avila, 160
+55 (21) 2287 4464
trousseau.com.br

5
Mobix, Lapa
Vintage Brazilian

For decades Rua do Lavradio has
been the go-to location for used
furniture and knick-knacks; it has
a street market dedicated to antiques
on the first Saturday of each month.
But in the past 10 years, a number
of high-end furniture stores have
opened and brought a more
discerning customer to the
neighbourhood. Italian-Brazilian
Arthur Cavaliere was one of the first
with a more upmarket offering.
   "The pieces are great examples
of Brazilian design from the 1950s,
'60s and '70s," says Cavaliere. His
inventory reads like a who's who of
the country's top talent with pieces
by Ricardo Fasanello, Joaquim
Tenreiro, Jorge Zalszupin and
the ubiquitous Sérgio Rodrigues.
"I don't just carry signed pieces,
though," says Cavaliere. "There are
also anonymous designs from this
period that are very beautiful."
Rua do Lavradio, 128
+55 (21) 2224 0244
mobixmoveis.com.br

7
Cerámica Luiz Salvador, Gávea
Blue period

Established in 1952 by Portuguese
ceramicist Luiz Salvador, the studio
that still bears his name – based in
the Petrópolis region of Rio de
Janeiro state – is famed for the high
glazes and delicate decoration of its
handcrafted plates, vases and table
lamps. The 2016 collection features
a distinctive blue-and-turquoise
colour palette and includes a
full dinner service plus a bold,
oversized flower vase. No need
to wait for a factory tour: head
to the third floor of Gávea's
shopping precinct.
*Shopping da Gávea, Rua Marquês
de São Vicente, 52*
+55 (21) 2422 2445
ceramicaluizsalvador.com.br

Does it make
me look like
a penguin?

⑧
Gabinete Duilio Sartori,
Jardim Botânico
Emerging homegrown talent

When, in 2009, Duilio Sartori and business partner Carlos Henrique Bertini bought the building that now houses their design shop it was completely abandoned and the floor was flooded. "When we cleared it out and uncovered the walls we found a beautiful space with historic Portuguese-made bricks," says Bertini.

The pair have transformed the space in the Jardim Botânico district into the best shop in the city for little-known Brazilian designers and craftspeople. You'll find unique paper items by Domingos Tótora, Regina Medeiros's glassware, leatherwork by Espedito Seleiro and lamps from Rio-based Cesar Burgos.

Sartori and Bertini are constantly travelling the country looking for new artisans and designers. The result, as Bertini explains, is a large collection of homegrown products, many of them exclusive. "Around 70 to 80 per cent of the items in the shop are by Brazilian designers; some of them you won't find on sale anywhere else."
Rua Lopes Quintas, 87
+55 (21) 3173 8828
gabineteduiliosartori.com.br

⑨
Shopping dos Antiquários,
Copacabana
Carnival of arcana

Although the real name of this historic retail centre is Shopping Cidade Copacabana, no one calls it that: it's dubbed the "antique mall" due to its eccentric second floor. This establishment has become a foraging ground for collectors, decorators and anyone with an eye for treasure. Stepping inside is like going back in time; the space is filled with antiques shops selling bric-a-brac of every variety. There's everything from chandeliers and Persian rugs to crockery and giant mirrors with gilt frames.
Rua Siqueira Campos, 143
shoppingdosantiquarios.com

⑩
Studio Zanini, Santo Cristo
Family fortunes

Zanini de Zanine was born in Rio in 1978 and became one of the most celebrated figures in Brazilian furniture design. Named designer of the year in 2015 by Maison & Objet Americas, De Zanine's creations are now classics in living rooms around the world. Among his most striking recent pieces are a set of jaunty, angular salt-and-pepper shakers and the Poltrona H 1950 armchair, which was restyled from an original concept by his father José (a celebrated furniture designer in his own right) and made from Madeira cariniana wood.
Rua Pedro Alves, 197
+55 (21) 2233 5061/7293
studiozanini.com.br

Bespoke style
——
Most products are by Brazilian designers

①
Granado, Centro
Time and lotion

Founded in 1870 by the
Portuguese chemist José Antônio
Coxito Granado, the boutique
that continues to bear his name
remains the most respected
soap and lotion purveyor in Rio.
Granado – now owned by the UK
entrepreneur Christopher Freeman
– still makes skin- and haircare
products, including Brazil-nut
shampoo, conditioner made from
herbs and witch-hazel hand cream.
Granado's unguents and
shampoos can also be found in
the bathrooms of Rio's plushest
hotels and restaurants.
Rua Primeiro de Março, 16
+ 55 (21) 3231 6746
granado.com.br

②
Havaianas, Ipanema
Flip-flop fillip

The ubiquitous Havaianas flip -flop,
introduced in 1962 and based on
the Japanese zori sandal, is probably
Brazil's most iconic fashion design;
more than 180 million pairs are sold
in more than 80 countries every
year. Manufacturer Alpargatas was
established in 1907 and is now the
leader in South America's shoe
market. There are countless colour
variations to choose from and
special designs from names such
as Missoni and Valentino. Purchase
from the Ipanema shop and you
can head straight to the beach
suitably attired.
Rua Visconde de Pirajá, 310
+ 55 (21) 2247 4713
havaianas.com

③
Toca do Vinicius, Ipanema
Bossa nova central

Bossa nova is a genre that originated
in Rio and is synonymous with it.
A mix of Brazilian samba and early
20th-century jazz, it became globally
popular in the 1950s and 1960s with
songs that even today scream Rio;
"The Girl from Ipanema" is the
most famous example.
    Carlos Alberto Afonso set up
this record shop dedicated to bossa
nova in 1993 and originally named
it Toca da Bossa Nova ("Den of
Bossa Nova"). But he decided
to change the name to include a
reference to the poet and chief
lyricist of bossa nova, Vinicius de
Moraes. You'll find Afonso, now in
his sixties, sitting at the back of his
shop surrounded by hundreds of
dusty books about the leading lights
of the genre. Ask him a question
and he'll regale you with anecdotes
and stories about his idols: Moraes,
Tom Jobim and João Gilberto.
Rua Vinicius de Moraes, 129
+ 55 (21) 2247 5227
tocadovinicius.com.br

I like to listen to a little bossa nova while I shop. Who doesn't?

④
Chapelaria Alberto, Centro
Traditional headwear

This hat retailer run by Luís Eduardo Fadel sits on the corner of a busy downtown street in a Portuguese colonial building. It's the perfect place to learn about Panama hats, which are actually made in Ecuador but became popular with workers during the construction of the Panama Canal far to the north. Panamas are sought-after all year round thanks to Rio's climate. The shop has adapted its business model over the years – it now has an online shop – but it still stays loyal to its traditional hat-sizing process.
Rua Buenos Aires, 73
+55 (21) 2252 9939
chapelariaalberto.com.br

⑤
Ao Bandolim de Ouro, Centro
Handcrafted instruments

This family-run business manufactures mandolins, banjos and *cavaquinhos* for top-level sambistas such as Paulinho da Viola. The instruments made here are handcrafted and it can take the firm's craftsmen up to three months to perfectly shape, sand and polish their pieces. Recently the business was included as part of Rio de Janeiro's heritage foundation in an attempt to keep its traditions alive and help preserve one of Brazil's strongest cultural offerings: samba. Prices for instruments start at R$1,000.
Praça da República, 75
+55 (21) 2233 2396
aobandolimdeouro.com.br

Heritage shops

In June 2013, in anticipation of the World Cup and the 2016 Summer Olympics, officials at Rio de Janeiro city hall decided to start protecting the city's heritage retailers. Thirteen businesses were added to the list in early 2015, bringing the total in the initiative to about 40.

The musical instrument manufacturer Ao Bandolim de Ouro and the dress-shirt and hat store Chapelaria Alberto (*see left*) are both part of the scheme. As is Charutaria Syria, a tobacco-shop-turned-wine-store that was founded in 1912. It is on Rua Senhor dos Passos in the heart of Saara, an area so called because of its large population of Arab immigrants (Charutaria Syria is named after the birthplace of the neighbourhood's founder).

Brazilian not-for-profit Sebrae firm has been assisting these 40 retailers by sharpening up their marketing, updating their administration processes and rethinking their brands. Protecting these heritage businesses is a crucial part of the city's plan to revitalise Rio's historic centre.

String theory
—
Samba music often features guitars

Nature appreciation

Rio de Janeiro has been classified as a Unesco World Heritage site since 2012. Aside from man-made wonders such as Jardim Botânico, the listing recognises the Parque Nacional da Tijuca, Corcovado Mountain and the hills around Guanabara Bay.

⑥ Oba!, Jardim Botânico
Premium toys

Leila Bittencourt is an architect by trade and her practice has developed a number of projects for children, including nurseries, playschools and kids' spaces in malls. In 2007 she decided to set up her own shop for children's toys and furniture and Oba! followed in 2013. It is one of only a handful of Rio retailers selling high-end products for children. Bittencourt regularly travels to São Paulo to pick up new pieces. "I wouldn't say these items are just for children: they're also for adults," she says. "I want them to be inspirational."
Rua Lopes Quintas, 147
+55 (21) 2249 5876
obaarquitetura.com.br

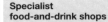

Sweet design

One of Aquim's most unusually shaped chocolate bars was designed by architect Oscar Niemeyer. Sadly, the collaboration has ended and the wonderfully curved Q10 confectionery bars are no longer available (although you can still buy the same chocolate in other shapes).

⑦ Aquim, Ipanema
Q branch

Founded and managed by the Italian-Portuguese Aquim family, this boutique chocolate shop sells delicate treats made from cocoa beans grown on the Fazenda Leolinda farm at Ilheus in Brazil's northeast. Everything in the shop is manufactured using a special process pioneered by the family and each recipe contains only pure cocoa, a pinch of sugar and cocoa butter. The Q Chocolate's jungle-chic packaging, designed by Claudio Novaes, has also been lauded: it received the Design Bronze Lion in Cannes.
Rua Garcia d'Avila, 149
+55 (21) 2274 1001
aquimgastronomia.com.br

Specialist food-and-drink shops

Shopping in Rio isn't just about buying bikinis and *sungas*: you might want to pick up some Brazilian delicacies as well.

01 Casa Carandaí, Jardim Botânico: This well-stocked grocery-store-cum-deli on leafy Rua Lopes Quintas is the perfect place for treats such as *goiabada*, a guava jelly often eaten with cheese as a delicious dessert.
casacarandai.com.br

02 Gaia Art & Café, Leme: Owner Flavia Torga has teamed up with Junta Local, a collective supporting producers from the Rio region, in order to offer products in her café on Rua Gustavo Sampaio. Every 15 days five new producers are invited to "occupy" the shelves.
gaiaartcafe.com

03 A Garrafeira, Leblon: This wine shop in the heart of Leblon's culinary district is a great place to pick up a bottle of sparkling wine or Brazilian red. Why not try a tipple from vineyard Cave Geisse?
agarrafeira.com.br

Did someone say award-winning chocolate?

Bookshops
Rio covered

② Argumento, Leblon
Opinions for the masses

This charming retailer has certainly earned its name: it was founded in São Paulo in 1978 during Brazil's military dictatorship and was a place for intellectuals, journalists and students to buy books on social sciences in a time of strict censorship. Argumento was the idea of Dalva Gasparian, who started the store following years in exile in the UK. Her husband was a lecturer in South American politics and economics at the University of Oxford.

Today Dalva's daughter Laura runs Argumento alongside her two brothers Eduardo and Marcus. The bookshop still has a leaning towards social sciences but you'll also find bestsellers and art-and-design books on the shelves. There's also the lovely Café Severino hidden at the back of the shop with a great selection of cakes and sandwiches.
Rua Dias Ferreira, 417
+55 (21) 2239 5294
livrariaargumento.com.br

Sabor Literário, Leblon
Word perfect

Located inside a small, rather unremarkable shopping centre in Leblon, this large glass rotunda is one of the more romantic of Rio's bookshop. Floor-to-ceiling shelves hold a huge variety of Brazilian publications from fiction to history, alongside Brazilian magazines.

At one end of the shop among the bookcases are a handful of sleek wooden dining tables with a small coffee bar serving lunch (with a daily menu of stews, soups and salads) and sweet treats. A rooftop space is often open for special events.
Rua Conde Bernadotte, 26
+55 (21) 2540 7935

① Livraria da Travessa, Botafogo
Architectural adventure

Travessa is one of Rio's most successful independent bookshop chains with seven outlets across the city (plus one in São Paulo). The Botafogo branch on Voluntários da Pátria is housed in a converted building that dates back to the start of the 20th century. The renovation was carried out by Brazilian architect Bel Lobo and there's a tiled floor, high ceilings and a garden space used for book-signings and talks. Choose one of the 60,000 books lining the shelves and grab a coffee at the cosy Focaccia Café, located on the mezzanine.
Voluntários da Pátria, 97
+55 (21) 3195 0200
travessa.com.br

Things we'd buy
—— Brazilian beachside bounty

It might seem perverse to go to Rio and spend your time strolling around a shopping district or an air-conditioned mall. But it's worth preparing for a day or two of rain during your stay – they do happen. And no matter how much you're enjoying the beach you will still want to take home some mementos.

We've gathered up these colourful trinkets and Brazilian-made clothes and design items so you know what's worth buying. And if you really can't drag yourself away from Rio's golden sands, we've included some tokens you'll be able to pick up from the beach vendors with your feet still in the surf.

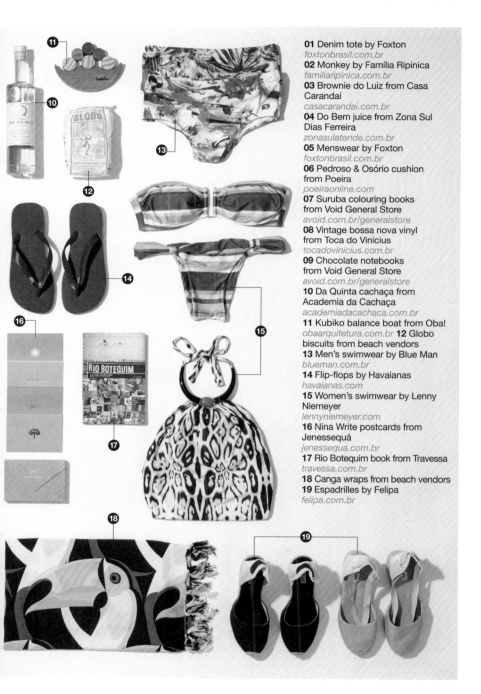

01 Denim tote by Foxton
foxtonbrasil.com.br
02 Monkey by Família Ripinica
familiaripinica.com.br
03 Brownie do Luiz from Casa Carandaí
casacarandai.com.br
04 Do Bem juice from Zona Sul Dias Ferreira
zonasulatende.com.br
05 Menswear by Foxton
foxtonbrasil.com.br
06 Pedroso & Osório cushion from Poeira
poeiraonline.com
07 Suruba colouring books from Void General Store
avoid.com.br/generalstore
08 Vintage bossa nova vinyl from Toca do Vinícius
tocadovinicius.com.br
09 Chocolate notebooks from Void General Store
avoid.com.br/generalstore
10 Da Quinta cachaça from Academia da Cachaça
academiadacachaca.com.br
11 Kubiko balance boat from Oba!
obaarquitetura.com.br **12** Globo biscuits from beach vendors
13 Men's swimwear by Blue Man
blueman.com.br
14 Flip-flops by Havaianas
havaianas.com
15 Women's swimwear by Lenny Niemeyer
lennyniemeyer.com
16 Nina Write postcards from Jenessequá
jenessequa.com.br
17 Rio Botequim book from Travessa
travessa.com.br
18 Canga wraps from beach vendors
19 Espadrilles by Felipa
felipa.com.br

01 Dried banana with cinnamon by Casa Carandaí
casacarandai.com.br
02 Caladryl after-sun lotion from Drogarias Pacheco
drogariaspacheco.com.br
03 Cosmetics by Granado
granado.com.br
04 Wooden plate by Gabinete Duilio Sartori
gabineteduiliosartori.com.br
05 Hipoglos multi-use cream

from Drogarias Pacheco
drogariaspacheco.com.br
06 Futah towel from Void
avoid.com.br
07 *Rio* by Marc Ferrez from Instituto Moreira Salles
ims.com.br
08 Q Chocolate by Aquim
chocolateq.com
09 Ceramic cup by Alice Felzenszwalb from Poeira
poeiraonline.com

10 Flamengo football jersey by Clube de Regatas do Flamengo
flamengo.com.br
11 Box of boxes by Gabinete Duilio Sartori
gabineteduiliosartori.com.br
12 *Inside Rio* by Michael Roberts from Travessa
travessa.com.br
13 Womenswear by Farm
farmrio.com.br

12 essays
—— Read all about Rio

*So many
stories to
read on
the beach*

Join the club
*The city that welcomes all
(just watch your wallet)*

***

**Rocky starts are
soon forgotten as the
unwavering charm of
Rio turns even the most
unlikely gringo into a
contented Carioca.**

*By Josh Fehnert,
Monocle*

May I be candid? My first visit to Rio de Janeiro started as a nervous one. My bags bulged with warm clothes not suited to the climate (and a stack of ill-advised collared shirts) to undertake a magazine assignment. "*Todo bem*?" said the taxi driver as his car purred to a stop at the arrivals terminal of low-slung Galeão International Airport. "Hello," I said in a plummy voice – immediately betraying my terrible grasp of Portuguese – as I scrabbled to find the address of my apartment, scrawled in large letters on a scrap of paper.

On the way into town the taxi window revealed clumps of shabby houses, hairy with makeshift electrical wiring, abutted by unfriendly concrete hoardings. The city felt alien and unknown. I felt uneasy. "Don't wear a watch out," people had said. "Listen out for gunshots," warned others. Nearby a helicopter hung low in the sky as its steady searchlight darted down the warren of alleys in a favela that flitted past the car window. I couldn't have felt more like a gringo.

For all its charm, Rio is more complicated than its postcard-perfect beaches. It's a complex, diverse city of 6.3 million souls – and it can be intimidating, even dicey. Although the pacification of its favelas has helped police re-establish control of some of the city's most lawless 'hoods, the wise rightly eschew unwanted attention and keep jewellery and wads of reais out of sight.

For me, after a few days the agitation passed. Talking to Cariocas, walking the city's streets and embarking on a few nerve-settling night-time sojourns to Lapa and Botafogo, it it was clear that Rio is worthy of its fun-loving reputation. It is a place where time passes contentedly on Ipanema Beach under the shadow of Dois Irmãos and cool cups of Matte Leão tea from beach vendors are replaced by punchy caipirinhas come nightfall.

I came to understand that the city's charm lies in its diversity. The veiled danger is as much a part of it as the breathless hedonism of a samba song or the scantily clad beauties of Rio's bounteous beaches. There was also no need to feel like a foreigner. Unlike many South American nations, Brazil's past has given rise to a multicultural citizenry who are used to change and whose past has been defined by the successive waves of gringos that made it unique.

Rio is home to the descendants of indigenous tribes, Portuguese colonisers,

**Three places to
feel like a Carioca**

***

01 Mirante do Leblon
Beaches bordered by favelas.
Contrast epitomised.
02 Lapa by night
A portal to the fun-loving city's
after-dark delights.
03 Christ the Redeemer
A cliché but a spectacular one
with views.

African slaves and newer Asian migrants. Its make-up means it is tough to gauge who's a gringo and who isn't. Svelte blonde waifs and elderly Asian couples share the title "Carioca" with swarthy European-looking sorts and Afro-Brazilians. In other cities my UK pallor may have betrayed me as an interloper but Cariocas are a diverse and welcoming bunch who are slow to judge.

This quirk of history and culture is an unexpected passport to the heart of what makes Rio such a vibrant city. It's a riotous melee of dancing and danger, of frivolity and favelas and of cheekiness and charm. From the winding, swirling Roberto Burle Marx-designed pavements of Copacabana to the steps that lead to the magnificent Christ the Redeemer statue (its breathtaking topography notwithstanding), Rio's openness and unique mix of people are what ultimately make it intoxicating and unique.

"The veiled danger is as much a part of it as the breathless hedonism of a samba song"

Come the end of the trip I reprised my airport taxi ride. As the sun lolled low in the sky, the yellow cab slowed at the departures terminal. "*Boa viagem,*" said the taxi driver. "*Obrigado,*" I responded before asking for a "*recibo*" (receipt) and wishing him well, like a man who's lived in the city all his life. Rio is a place that doesn't hide away from its charms – or its wrinkles – so don't be nervous about its reputation (but please do be sensible, of course). No matter what your preconceptions, it's blissfully simple to feel like a Carioca and that's a wonderful title to hold. — (M)

ABOUT THE WRITER: Josh Fehnert is MONOCLE's Edits editor. He visited Rio in 2013 to co-edit a travel guide for the magazine. He's been hankering for one of barman Paulo Freitas's cocktails at Bar Astor, opposite Ipanema's Posto 8, ever since.

ESSAY 02

Class dismissed
Boundary-breaking beaches

———

More than a spot for a surf and a sunbathe, the beach is the heartbeat of the city, where economic divisions are left at the door.

By Gaia Lutz, Monocle

Yes, Rio's unusual mixture of white fluffy beaches, glistening water and imposing, forest-covered mountains is probably the biggest reason tourists visit the city in their droves. It's also why Cariocas living abroad (like myself) miss it so much. But I would argue that there is more to Rio's beaches than to those found anywhere else in the world.

As a local I would advise visitors heading to Rio for a tranquil retreat on which to read a book to turn around and look elsewhere. Beaches in Rio are far from quiet and peaceful but all the better for it. You can, of course, find any number of remote and secluded spots on one of the 59 stretches of sand spread out along the city's 170km of arresting coastline – but those are not the spots that make Rio, well… Rio.

As any trip to one of the city's beaches at the weekend will quickly show you, this is where life unfolds. It is where you get your summer tan and your daily exercise. It is where children build sandcastles, teenagers hang out and adults unwind, beer in hand. You can indulge in a caipirinha from one of its many kiosks and then soothe your throat with a fresh coconut water afterwards. Vendors compete with one another with creative and ever-louder chants as they ply their wares, including corn on the cob, ice creams, *kibbes* (meat croquettes) and vegetarian burgers – all of which can be consumed right there on the sand.

> *"Businessman and garbage man, man and woman, all are equal and naked"*

Cariocas often insist that their beaches are the city's most democratic spaces; that the sands of Copacabana and Ipanema heal the city's many divisions; that the super-wealthy and the penniless, the businessman and the garbage man, man and woman, are all equal and naked (almost, at least) under the Rio sun. Although there are some flaws in this argument – beaches in affluent neighbourhoods will invariably attract a more well-heeled crowd – there is also an element of truth to it.

Unlike on the sands of the French Riviera, there are no fixed tents here

Best beachside spots to watch the sunset

01 The rocks in Arpoador
If the sunset is spectacular, it gets a round of applause.
02 Gávea Beach Club
Eat gourmet nibbles while watching the hang-gliders.
03 Confeitaria Colombo, Forte de Copacabana
Reserve a table.

that guarantee better spots to those with more weight in their wallets. In Rio the policy is strictly first come, first served. For a notoriously chauvinist society it might surprise some to see both boys and girls playing *altinha* (a game that involves keeping a football in the air without the use of one's hands) together all along the waterfront.

If there are divisions on the beaches of Rio they are not carved along strictly socioeconomic lines. Instead people arrange themselves into groups depending on other factors. The many *postos* (numbered sectors marking every kilometre of the coastline) informally appeal to different tribes: Posto 7 is the surfers' spot, while the area between 8 and 9 has a rainbow flag flying high, signalling a gay-friendly zone. Posto 9 has a younger, more liberal crowd, whereas Posto 12 has managed to attract a clientele of families with small children because of a single kiosk owner's ingenious idea of setting up a nappy-changing point and playground.

People born in Rio experience the world in relation to the sea. As a

Carioca, whether you are a beach-lover or not, you innately know the expression "*Mormaço queima*", or "Even the hot air can burn you" (something many gringos are unaware of, insisting on not applying sunscreen on cloudy days).

As a Carioca, you know how to tan without ending up with any awkward tanlines. You get your bearings by knowing that a street always slopes down towards the sea. You know how to *pegar jacaré*, or to surf a wave using your body as stiff as a surfboard and you have mastered the skill of cleaning your sandy feet without using water.

People in Rio often talk about the varying scents of the *maresia*, or sea air, rather than the weather. Cariocas know that the best cure for a hangover is a dive in the ocean followed by a fresh coconut water. The girls know how to nimbly tie a *canga*, or beach towel, around their bodies in a fashionable way and the men never cease to find new ways of comparing a woman's eyes to the sea. The beach is as much a part of the Carioca as the Carioca is part of the beach.

So if you're tempted to bypass the beach in favour of a day spent sightseeing or imbibing the local culture, don't overlook the possibility of doing both with your feet buried in sand. Only in Rio. — (M)

ABOUT THE WRITER: Gaia Lutz is a researcher for MONOCLE and a Carioca. She now lives in London but her heart is still somewhere in the sands of Ipanema. On a rainy day she commutes to work on the Underground to the sound of bossa nova.

ESSAY 03
Built to order
An eclectic city centre

Downtown Rio is a symphony of architecture on a grand stage; this is where you'll find baroque cathedrals that are as much at home as modernist museums.

*By Claudia Moreira Salles,
designer*

Urban life in Rio started in the Centro district and, despite the expansion of the city in all directions, it remains the best illustration of the country's various historical periods. For me, as a designer and a Carioca, there is no better place in Rio to understand the city's history and its architecture. Although this is a city of so much natural beauty, it's the built environment of Centro – its houses, squares and streets – that have been the key part of my visual education.

As a child in the 1960s I started going to this neighbourhood with my parents to attend mass on Sundays in a baroque church, Nossa Senhora do Carmo. There were other churches where we lived but the ritual and the spiritualism were enhanced here by the glitz and the grandiosity of its white-and-gold interiors. The church is on Praça XV, one of Rio's landmarks and one charged with history. Also on the square is the Paço Imperial, the seat of the Portuguese court when it

Best builds

01 Edifício Gustavo Capanemo
Masterpiece on stilts.
02 Casa França Brasil
Opulent neoclassical interiors.
03 Real Gabinete Português de Leitura
Neo-gothic library with hand-carved wooden bookshelves.

transferred to Brazil in 1808. Leaving the baroque decor on a Sunday, I was always impressed by the contrast with this relatively simple construction, all pristine white, punctuated by doors and windows and framed by grey granite. It was minimalism *avant la lettre*.

After that it was off for an ice cream at Confeitaria Colombo, an example of Brazil's tropical version of the belle epoque style. On our way back we would pass in front of the Museu de Arte Moderna, the Mam (*see page 105*), one of the most beautiful examples of Carioca modernism. In 1974 the museum hosted an exhibition about the Bauhaus movement that was one of the key reasons I later chose design as a career.

When I was 12 years old my school organised a visit to the Ministry of Education and Culture, otherwise known as the Palácio Gustavo Capanema – another striking moment in my aesthetic education. Construction on the building started in 1936 and it was finished in 1945. The team of architects included Lucio Costa, Oscar Niemeyer, Affonso Eduardo Reidy and Roberto Burle Marx for the gardens – all the heavyweights of Rio design.

Once I got past the intimidation of visiting a place associated with authority (this was during the military regime) I was lost in wonder walking through the spaces between the elegant, high pilotis that hold up the 16-storey building. I hadn't been to Greece but I imagined this was akin to walking through ancient temples. On one side there was a white-and-blue *azulejo* (tile) panel, a reference to Portuguese architecture on a monumental scale, designed by Candido Portinari.

I had been to modernist residences and public buildings before but this one was outstanding. I knew each corner would surprise me. You don't need to have knowledge of architectural vocabulary to understand and feel a place is unique and that beauty is fundamental.

Years later, having studied at the Escola Superior de Desenho Industrial (Esdi), the design school in the neighbourhood of Lapa, I was accepted as a trainee at the design institute of the Mam. Every afternoon I left Lapa and walked to work across a footbridge with the most graceful curve. The museum, moreover, has one of the most beautiful modernist spiral staircases in Rio and through its windows you can see the mountains of Guanabara Bay. Every Carioca's aesthetics are shaped by curves like these and mine are no exception.

During the 1980s a renovation programme was begun, which gave renewed life to a number of public buildings in Centro: the Paço Imperial, Banco do Brasil and the old port-customs headquarters, an elegant neoclassical-style building that today is the Casa França-Brasil (I had my first solo furniture exhibition here in 1998). They have become cultural centres dedicated to the arts. Today Lapa is a nightlife destination with bars and places to dance and listen to good music, all occupying restored old townhouses. Some were torn down and I recall going with my mother as a child, hunting for *azulejos* that were sold by the demolition teams.

Every now and then, and for very different reasons, urbanists, architects and

> *"I find neighbourhoods where the old and the new coexist by far the most interesting"*

politicians attempt to interfere in the city. In 1921, for instance, Morro do Castelo, a hill in the centre of Rio that had been inhabited for centuries, was razed to the ground by mayor Carlos Sampaio, who worried that the hill prevented clean air from sweeping into the city. The Aterro do Flamengo (*see page 115*) irrevocably changed the shoreline of Guanabara Bay – but brought with it a large park, beautifully designed by Burle Marx.

A raised highway, the Perimetral, was recently destroyed as part of the revitalisation of the port zone, itself a massive project. Two new museums have already sprung up in this area: the Museu do Mar by Thiago Bernardes and Paulo Jacobsen and the Museu do Amanhã by Santiago Calatrava. I find neighbourhoods where the old and the new coexist by far the most interesting and Centro is where this symbiosis is most obvious. All the urban changes that have taken place here over the centuries show how daring, how open to new ideas and how proud of their city Cariocas are. — (M)

ESSAY 04
Fill your boots
Derby day at the Maracanã

———

Long before the ref signals kick-off, earnest cries of allegiance bellow through the stadium. Sundays at the Maracanã are for Rio's most devout.

By Matt Alagiah, Monocle

We've taken our seats in the top tier of the Estádio do Maracanã. It's 15 minutes until kick-off and already the fans are on their feet, or standing on their chairs, chanting in unison and bouncing up and down as one amorphous mass. The drumming has started and the low, regular beats shudder up through the concrete stand.

Through the oval slit in the roof it's possible to make out the tropical vegetation on the hills of the nearby Parque Nacional da Tijuca. However, as night sets in and the floodlights come on, this backdrop loses its definition and becomes simply a huge looming darkness hanging over the stadium, creating the atmosphere of an amphitheatre. In spite of its vast size and the crowds crammed into it, the Maracanã still manages to feel intimate, even claustrophobic.

We're here to watch Fla-Flu, the biggest derby match in Rio club football: Flamengo, traditionally seen as the people's team, the team of the working

ABOUT THE WRITER: Born in Rio de Janeiro, Claudia Moreira Salles is a furniture designer whose products are strongly influenced by the Brazilian mid-century tradition. Although she moved to São Paulo in the 1980s for professional reasons, she still frequently travels to Rio to work and regain energy. Every time the plane approaches Guanabara Bay, she has the impression she is coming home.

classes and the favelas, up against Fluminense, conventionally the team of the privileged and the wealthy.

Ten minutes before kick off and a whisper goes around the stand: "Raça is here." Raça Rubro-Negra is one of the many fan clubs that support Flamengo and it is, by all accounts, the biggest and one of the oldest. The Raça members cluster together in one part of the stand, lead their own chants and have a series of enormous flags that they wave throughout the match; one features a grim-faced, muscular-armed vulture (the Flamengo mascot) above the words "Raça: *Desde* [since] 1977".

In fact, if you take the time to look around the Flamengo stands, you realise there are countless smaller fan clubs dotted about the stadium, sects in a broad church, displaying their allegiance with an idiosyncratic piece of clothing or gesture. Close to where we're sitting, for example, there's a Fla-*moeda* flag (*Desde* 2006); the slogan simply means "Fla-coin" and no one seems to understand the meaning. There's the group, apparently the "new generation" of fans, all wearing yellow hats; further away there's another waving small black-and-red chequered flags; and further still there's a group that blows up white balloons and waves them in the air above their heads just after kick-off.

> "For football fans around the world, visiting the Maracanã feels like the culmination of a pilgrimage. If the game has a spiritual home, it's here"

The Flamengo fans are renowned throughout the world for the volume of their singing and the passion they bring to each week's encounter. As we wait in anticipation for the referee's first whistle, it's easy to see why. There is not a moment's pause in the anthems, each chant following directly on the heels of

Game-changers

01 Fluminense v Flamengo (1963)
Historical final with 0-0 result.
02 Santos v Vasco de Gama (1969)
Pelé scores his 1,000th goal.
03 Flamengo v Botafogo (1989)
Zico scores his final and 333rd goal for Flamengo.

the one before and each just as loud. In fact, according to footballing folklore, Maracanã Stadium has only been silenced three times in its history.

The first of these occasions came about at the 1950 World Cup, in a match that is still heralded as one of the most extraordinary in the competition's history. The Maracanã, officially named after the popular Brazilian journalist Mário Filho, was built to be the main venue in this World Cup. The game in question was the decisive showdown between Uruguay and Brazil. Uruguay had managed to reach the final pool in impressive fashion but they were up against the comfortable favourites. Not only were Brazil playing at home in their new stadium but they were also considered the best team in the world with three exceptional forwards – Ademir, Chico and Zizinho – who had terrorised defences throughout the tournament.

Black-and-white photographs of the game show the players in their loose shirts and clunky-looking boots completely dwarfed against the quite extraordinary background of the vast, teeming stands. The number of spectators watching the game in the Maracanã was officially a world-record crowd of 175,000 but according to estimates it was probably nearer 210,000. These contemporary photos really capture the density of the crowds – there is not an inch of spare space on those stands.

The Uruguayan winger Alcides Ghiggia ended up stunning the stadium – and simultaneously breaking millions of

Brazilian hearts – when his low shot in the 79th minute put his team 2-1 ahead. Uruguay won the game against all the odds. And when he later looked back on this single moment in an astonishing game, he said, "Only three people have silenced the Maracanã: Frank Sinatra, the pope and me."

I can easily believe that it hasn't been silenced again since. Tonight the noise is deafening, even though the result itself is never really in doubt. Emerson Sheik puts Flamengo ahead on nine minutes to rapturous celebrations: then Kayke virtually seals the game with another goal in the 15th. Fluminense's Jean manages to pull one back in the 58th minute but a well-worked goal in the 69th sees Flamengo home to a comfortable win. No matter – the singing continues throughout, with barely a pause for breath.

For football fans around the world, visiting the Maracanã feels like the culmination of a pilgrimage. If the beautiful game has a spiritual home, it's here on the turf of the so-called *templo sagrado* of Brazilian football. But what's really wonderful is that for the people of Rio, this is close to an every-Sunday occurrence. Tickets can be picked up for as little as R$30 which, while still remaining out of the reach of some, allows even some of Rio's poorest families to witness the spectacle live. All the proof you need comes at the end of the game. As the match draws to a satisfying close and the Fluminense stands rapidly empty, a rousing Flamengo chant raises the roof of the Maracanã: "*Festa na favela*" ("Party in the favela"). — (M)

ABOUT THE WRITER: Matt Alagiah is MONOCLE'S Business editor and spent 10 days in Rio reporting for this guide. While he enjoyed unbuttoning his mandatory cardigan and walking along the sands of Copacabana Beach, the highlight of his trip was the match at the Maracanã Stadium.

ESSAY 05
Next on the menu
Rio's culinary shift

————

Cariocas are getting creative in the kitchen. Long-loved staples are being reimagined, propelling Brazilian cuisine onto fine diners' plates.

By Donna Bowater, writer

Lunch in Rio is a satisfyingly no-frills affair. It's less an opportunity for fine dining and more a functional meal to satisfy the hunger of a hectic tropical city. Come noon on any working day Rio slows down, loosens its tie and gorges on a usually hearty but humble meal, or *prato executivo*.

Almost every canteen-style restaurant with plastic-covered tables advertises similar cheap-and-cheerful fare on streetside whiteboards. The dish of the day, every day, is grilled steak, chicken or fish with the standard carb-heavy accompaniments: black beans, rice and a crunchy flour called *farofa*, made from the abundant manioc root. The bustling diners are busy early with hungry locals from every walk of life who chatter as they fill up for the rest of the day.

But while traditional Brazilian food is fundamentally simple, based on its native crops and prepared in an unpretentious fashion, there is a growing appetite for more sophisticated cuisine. As Rio's burgeoning middle class gentrifies some of its southern neighbourhoods, such conventional staples have been reimagined for the aspirational classes. From the famous lime-and-liquor cocktail caipirinha to the Brazilian beef cut *picanha*, the classics have gone gourmet as young, entrepreneurial restaurateurs experiment with home-grown flavours.

In just three years in the affluent area of Botafogo – lying between Sugarloaf Mountain and Christ the Redeemer – I have seen the mandatory collection of simple bars and *botecos* joined by more fashionable new venues. Now, instead of a glass of fresh juice from any corner joint, I can also visit Mahalo, a Hawaiian-styled bar, for a Hawaiian Detox: a blend of melon, pineapple and mint. In addition to snacking on a R$5 cheese-and-ham crepe made on the roadside from tapioca flour, I can also enjoy bite-size tapioca cubes prepared with cheese curd and served with watermelon jelly and rocket pesto at The Boua Kitchen Bar, a pub with its own microbrewery.

Even the cheap chocolate sweet of Brazilian childhoods has been reinvented. I have relived my own infancy in Rio enjoying the remnants of many a bowl of *brigadeiro*, marvelling at the heavenly simplicity of heating together a can of condensed milk and two heaped spoonfuls of chocolate powder to make a sticky ganache. But for the rising classes of Botafogo there is now also Brigadeiros do Tuiter, a kitsch café where you can enjoy an espresso and one of the endless varieties of *brigadeiro* in flavours ranging from carrot cake to pistachio and Belgian chocolate to cheesecake.

And it's not just in Botafogo. A trendy strip of cafés, bistros and bars has emerged in the leafy neighbourhood of Horto, close to the Jardim Botânico. It was here, at Bar do Horto, that I first tried a fruity *caipilé*: a creation based on the caipirinha – which is usually made with the cheap sugarcane spirit cachaça mixed with lime – but with a choice of different fruits, vodka and an ice lolly for added novelty. In Humaitá there is a hub of fashionable restaurants to explore, serving fusion food that mixes Brazilian flavours with European influences. One of my favourites is the beef stew in black beer with Brazil-nut rice and crunchy toasted *farofa* served up at Meza Bar.

Meanwhile, in the less-visited Zona Norte, the next generation of bar-owners are consciously modernising their *botecos*, where locals typically catch up over a cold beer and a plate of deep-fried bar snacks. Bar do Bode Cheiroso, close to the famous Maracanã Stadium, still offers traditional finger food, or *petiscos*, as well as more creative options for a largely white-collar clientele, such as crunchy prawns breaded in cashew nuts with passion-fruit jam and gorgonzola mayonnaise.

Rio is also enjoying a renaissance of street food. While the typical popcorn, tapioca and churros carts can still be found on every street corner, an increasing number of food bikes and trucks is also appearing, meeting the demand for artisan food at reasonable prices. Many of these are brought together in chic fairs or markets at events in Botafogo, Gávea and Glória, organised by O Cluster, a collective that unites independent fashion, food, music and art. Here, common Brazilian snacks such as *pão de queijo* (cheesy dough balls) are recreated as delicacies filled with cheese, rocket and sundried tomatoes or Parma ham, while the doughnut-like *sonho* has gained a status on a par with the designer cupcake.

"It is an exciting time to be an adventurous food-lover in Rio, where there is an increasingly diverse food scene"

It is an exciting time to be an adventurous food-lover in Rio, where

ESSAY 06

Welcome to the jungle
Rio's shady saviour

———

From the towering Imperial Palms to the balconies sprouting mini oases, Rio has a fervently green thumb.

By Andrew Tuck, Monocle

there is an increasingly diverse food scene. When I first arrived in Brazil I was keen to try all of the city's typical dishes including the national dish *feijoada*, a pork stew of off-cuts (ears, tail and feet are acceptable) borrowed from Portugal and turned Brazilian with the addition of those ubiquitous black beans. And after trying the most traditional meals, cooked with simplicity and humility, it's a discovery to see how staple foods can be reinvented. To appreciate Brazilian food is to understand where the country has come from and where it has arrived. It's a worthwhile journey through past to present, one that will leave visitors both satisfied and hungry for more. — (M)

OK, we all love a strip of sand and, even if your tootsies have never waded into the Atlantic waters of Ipanema or Leblon, you will have a pretty good impression from all the tourist promotions – and Mario Testino photoshoots – of life on a Brazilian beach. Yes, people really are that good-looking. But it's when you turn your attention 180 degrees from the ocean that another Rio reveals itself in all its fertile glory.

Walk away from the sand and within seconds you are under the cooling canopy of vast trees, where curtains of exotic greenery cascade from the apartment blocks. While the postcard image of Rio is all bleached sunlight and glistening heat, there is another city of shade and forest and

ABOUT THE WRITER: Donna Bowater is a UK journalist based in Rio de Janeiro, where she has reported on Brazil and South America for the English-language press since 2012.

Enjoying the greenery

01 Parque Large
Italian villa surrounded by beautiful European-style gardens.
02 Ipanema
Tropical, shady backstreets.
03 Aterro do Flamengo
Roberto Burle Marx's stunning coastal park.

crazy vegetation. The word fecund could have been grown for this city and, as you look up at the jungly mountains that surround the city, you see an army of trees that would clearly retake this urban outpost given half a chance.

It's the street shade that allows life to tick along; mass lethargy would rule supreme without this other, cooler city. Under the trees people walk their dogs (or get their maids or housekeepers to walk them), young mums take coffee outdoors without need for air-con and grandmothers go to the cornershop without fear of collapse. It's not only cooler here but the brightness is also held in check; in some places the sun is so filtered it dissipates to a dusk-like glow.

It's not surprising that one of the most celebrated names associated with the city is that of a landscape architect: the late Roberto Burle Marx. Although a son of São Paulo he is perhaps most famous for designing the mosaiced promenade in Copacabana. Burle Marx was the man enlisted by Brazil's modernist architects to landscape their new-world vision and his use of native

"It's the street shade that allows life to tick along; mass lethargy would rule supreme without this other, cooler city"

plants with architectural shapes has its most personal take here in Rio at his home in Guaratiba. Of course you should wander through this modest house packed to the rafters with his collections of pottery and figurines but it's the grounds of the former banana plantation that are worth the pilgrimage: there are literally thousands of specimens thrusting lustily from the soil.

Walk around Lagoa (where some towers seem to spring from the forest) or head back into Ipanema and the entrances to every apartment block and office building are packed with beds and pots of robust tropical planting that impress. It's the fact that when you look up, balconies are crammed with trees and orchids. Or how at street level, giant succulents flourish. It's the abundance that has a hold of this city and seems to demand so little caring or pampering to look its sexy best. But, hold on, are we talking plant or beach life now?
— (M)

ABOUT THE WRITER: Andrew Tuck is MONOCLE's editor and the presenter of various Monocle 24 shows, including *The Urbanist*, the show about the cities we live in. Tune in at *monocle.com* to hear tales from the city – including Rio, of course.

ESSAY 07
Life of the party
Carnival's block culture

———

Away from the quivering feathers and booming beats of the official samba parades lies a whole other side to Rio's Carnival. In every neighbourhood, on every street corner, the 'carnaval de rua' can tell you all you need to know about Rio, its residents and the city's psyche.

By Georgia Grimond, writer

To celebrate the arrival of Lent every year, Rio puts on two parallel but altogether different events. At the Sambadrome, thousands of Carnival dancers toe-tap their way down the concrete catwalk. Drums rat-tat-tat and unwieldy floats follow, draped in gaudy colours and laden with smiling, shimmying, samba-ing bodies. This is what the world knows as the "greatest show on Earth" – which indeed it is.

It is also a lucrative show. The official Carnival turns a healthy profit for the city as well as O Globo, Brazil's media giant which has the transmission rights. The competing samba schools stand to win cash (as well as glory) and tickets are sold to watch the spectacle each night. For a few hundred euros, tourists can buy a costume and join in the fray. For many thousands of euros, countries and companies can sponsor floats (though some of the samba schools are accused of funding their efforts with profits from illegal gambling). Not unlike the business of football, the more money a school has behind it, the better its float tends to do.

If the Sambadrome is the beating heart of the city during Carnival then the street parties, or *blocos*, are the blood that runs through its veins. For a month a year, Rio is awash with merry revellers marching through its neighbourhoods, parading loyally behind a band or soundsystem. There are close to 500 every year and each one has a different identity or theme that unites its followers. They are free and open to everyone and require nothing but good humour, stamina and ideally a fancy-dress costume.

Aside from the merriment, Carnival over the years has also given Cariocas a chance to air their views. One *bloco*, Banda de Ipanema, was founded during the first year of the country's military dictatorship in 1964. Democratic and irreverent, it mocked the new regime and unnerved the authorities with its meaningless motto, "Yolhesman Crisbeles". As the dictatorship started to crumble in the 1980s, Simpatia é Quase Amor (Sympathy is Almost Love) emerged on the streets. This group campaigned for direct elections and its marchers could be heard calling: "Hello, Ipanema bourgeoisie!" Today these are some of the biggest *blocos*, attracting hundreds of thousands of followers each year. And still throughout Carnival political slogans can be seen dotted among the crowds.

While some *blocos* have the weight of history behind them, others have their tongue in their cheek. Suvaco do Cristo, or Christ's Armpit, is so called because it marches through Jardim Botânico, a neighbourhood nestled under the right arm of Christ the Redeemer. Bunytos de Corpo (Beautiful Bodies) sprints through Centro, stopping traffic, with hundreds of lunging, stretching dancers clad in Lycra and neon 1980s sportswear. In Santa Teresa, men and women dressed in habits swarm the streets to honour the story of a Carmelite nun who jumped the convent wall to join Carnival. In the same neighbourhood, fans of the

Super Mario Bros can join an army of Marios and Luigis to mosey through the cobbled streets and hear the soundtrack of the video game played by a samba band.

Each *bloco* is defined by its music and I never fail to be impressed by the groups of Cariocas who come together, armed with drums and brass instruments, to tirelessly play the unrelenting soundtrack of Carnival. It is hard work in that heat. In the evenings when I hear my neighbour toot-tooting on his trumpet I secretly hope he is practicing to one day be part of a *bloco*.

Tracking through the city, the snakes of people morph to fit the streets, squeezing through narrow roads or spilling onto the beach or into a square. There are *blocos* for families, for kids, for gay people, even for dogs (so long as they are dressed up). There are no limits to what a *bloco* can be or who can start one; all that is needed is a permit from the city. In just a few years Sargento Pimenta, which plays samba Beatles songs, went from being an idea between a few friends to performing at the 2012 London Olympics closing ceremony.

Oh Ménage, however, doesn't bother with a permit. By changing its starting point every year it flies under the official radar and maintains its rebel status. It has been known to storm the domestic airport, leading its revellers up the escalators and back down and out again. The staff were seen singing along and the

Three top tips for Carnival
—
01 **Drink water and wear sun-cream**: the Brazilian sun is unforgiving.
02 **Try the sacolés:** reviving and delicious frozen fruit-flavoured caipirinha popsicles.
03 **Be ready to kiss:** Everyone does it.

supervisor merely shrugged the invasion off, saying there is nothing you can do about this kind of event.

That's the thing about Carnival: it is naughty and infectious and amusing. It pumps blood through the city, flooding dusty arteries with joyous music and rippling energy. The Cariocas who don't flee the chaos come out in force. Sometimes maligned the rest of the year for being apathetic, they quietly and thanklessly pull together to put on the show and make their voices heard. Friendships are formed, romances blossom (people born in November are jokingly known as "Carnival babies") and for visitors, it's the best way to see the Cidade Maravilhosa. Worm your way into the centre of a smaller *bloco* and get to know Rio, its streets and, most importantly, its people. — (M)

> *"In the evenings when I hear my neighbour toot-tooting on his trumpet I secretly hope he is practicing to one day be part of a 'bloco'"*

ABOUT THE WRITER: Georgia Grimond is a freelance journalist based in Rio. With four carnivals under her belt, her advice is to plan and pace yourself, and then escape to a quiet seaside spot to recuperate and nurse your *ressaca de Carnaval* – or carnival hangover.

ESSAY O8
Looking from a hilltop
The future of the favelas

———

No longer simply a thorn in Rio's side, favelas are an essential part of the city's ecosystem. But these neighbourhoods still face very real challenges.

By Christopher Frey, Monocle

Stories of poverty, drugs and violence: for too long these were all that outsiders ever heard of Rio's favelas, the only tales the media and popular culture deemed fit to tell. It's only in the past decade that the way favelas are portrayed and understood has begun to shift. Among city thinkers and social scientists they are now often praised as hubs of urban ingenuity, entrepreneurship and civic co-operation. Whether it's in music, art or the annual explosion of creativity around Carnival, the contributions of *favelados* to Rio's culture are rightly celebrated. Once demonised, colourful images of favela life are now used to sell Rio to tourists.

It might be fair to wonder whether sensationalism has yielded too far the other way, to romanticising the very real challenges that *favelados* still face. Today, 20 per cent of Cariocas live in one of 1,000 favelas, many of them occupying Rio's most extreme terrain: astride vertiginous hillsides, floodplains and even former landfills. Contrary to popular misconception they are neither slums nor shantytowns: most homes are made of brick or concrete and a majority enjoy electricity, running water and internet access. Many families have made generations' worth of investments in homes. Yet, they still lack for much.

By many measures living conditions in favelas have improved. Much of this is the product of the *favelados*' efforts, whether through work-training programmes offered by neighbourhood samba schools or cooperative credit initiatives. But more progressive attitudes in government have also helped.

> *"20 per cent of Cariocas live in one of 1,000 favelas, many of them occupying Rio's most extreme terrain"*

Overdue investments in infrastructure are making favelas better integrated with the city. Strong economic growth (until recently anyway) coupled with financial-assistance programmes have improved rates of upward social mobility: 65 per cent of Brazil's favela residents are now considered middle class by Brazilian standards, and they're recognised as a potent political force at the ballot box.

The authorities' biggest interventions, however, have proved more contentious. A "pacification" programme has ousted some of the drug gangs from the favelas they once controlled but has been slow to deliver the promised social services.

Perhaps it's worth remembering that the very first favela was born of a broken promise. In 1897, thousands of soldiers fresh from quashing a rebellion in the northeast of Brazil came streaming into Rio, where the government had assured them land. They discovered, of course, that no such land lay waiting for them. Left to fend for themselves they improvised a settlement atop Morro da Providência, a hill overlooking the city's docks. The veterans took to calling it a

Favela films
—
01 **City of God (2002)**
Kinetic crime drama about warring drug gangs circa 1970s.
02 **Bus 174 (2002)**
The story of an infamous Rio bus hijacking.
03 **Hill of Pleasures (2013)**
Low-key observational documentary about one favela post-pacification.

"favela" – after a prickly desert weed they encountered while fighting in the north.

It has often been noted that *favelados* have built more square feet of Rio than anyone else before or since. But today many of them feel as anxious as ever about their tenuous place in the city. In some pacified favelas, like Vidigal and Complexo do Alemão, rents have shot up two- or even three-fold, pricing out long-term residents. Outsiders are buying up property, opening hotels and bars for tourists; favela lofts with astonishing views now get snatched up on Airbnb. While the influx of money is often welcomed, gentrifying forces will likely end up testing the fabric of favela communities.

The process of integrating informal settlements with the rest of the city was always going to be messy, full of missteps, abuses and commitments unkept, with the *favelados* vigilantly fighting for a say in how their communities are transformed. It is probably Rio's defining story. At least now, there is finally a sense that favelas aren't simply a problem to be solved. Rather, they are starting to be seen as a place to go to find solutions. — (M)

ABOUT THE WRITER: MONOCLE's Toronto correspondent Christopher Frey once lived in the Santa Teresa neighbourhood. Listening to Tom Jobim's "Águas de Março" helps him through the long Canadian winters.

ESSAY 09

Cities divided
The Rio-São Paulo rivalry

———

Like quarrelling siblings, the citizens of Rio and São Paulo are constantly engaged in a spirited debate about which is Brazil's leading city. But at the end of the day, no love is lost.

By Fernando Augusto Pacheco, Monocle

The flight route between Rio de Janeiro and São Paulo, or the *ponte aérea* ("aerial bridge") as we say in Portuguese, is one of the busiest air routes in the world. Four million people used the route in 2014 alone, two million in each direction and about 78,000 people fly it every week. And in the somewhat chaotic world of Brazilian transport, the services on the *ponte aérea* usually run surprisingly smoothly. Every time I arrive for check-in on this flight, for instance, they ask me if I would like to board an earlier flight. Where else does that happen?

Yet despite the slick air connections and the crucial economic interdependence of these two cities, there is still fierce competition between them. As a Paulistano – someone from São Paulo – I was taught from an early age that the two cities are archrivals. And there is a firm foundation for this rivalry: the cities really couldn't be more different, from their size and geography to the way their residents dress. While Rio is literally shaped by nature – by its mountains, forests and coastline – São Paulo is purely an urban jungle. And while São Paulo feels like a sprawling metropolis with its 10 million inhabitants, Rio sometimes feels like a little village where everyone knows everyone else (even though it is in fact home to some 6.3 million). The differing architecture makes this visual mismatch even more obvious. São Paulo's high-rise apartment blocks and old-fashioned neoclassical buildings are in complete contrast to Rio's modernist vibes.

Culturally too there are huge differences. When it comes to music, Cariocas love their samba and their funk, while in São Paulo it's all about hip-hop and electronic dance, even country. When it comes to health and fitness, Paulistas will opt for a run on the treadmill and any kind of fad diet to lose weight; in Rio, everyone strives to have a muscular body that can be shown off on the beach all year round.

So until recently, every time someone asked me where I was from in Brazil, I replied saying that I was from São Paulo but I also always felt a bit defensive. I ended up saying things like: "It's not the prettiest city but we do have the best restaurants and the best nightlife, you know." It was, I can now confess, the result of a mix of jealousy and admiration for that other city, Rio de Janeiro, the one all the foreigners dream of visiting.

And who am I kidding? I am, of course, a big fan of Rio too. Every time I go back to Brazil, I hop on the *ponte aérea* and spend at least two days in the "Marvellous City" (as Cariocas like to call it; meanwhile, we Paulistanos can only

"Whatever Paulistanos say, we will always enjoy spending our weekends in Rio and, yes, we will even do our business there"

come up with rather less exciting names such as "Concrete City" or "Drizzle City" for our own hometown).

Now, when a foreigner asks me about Brazil, I wholeheartedly recommend a trip to Rio, saying it is worth visiting that it is a special city with almost divine geography. If there's time in the conversation I will of course add a thing or two about my town of São Paulo, but more just to say that it's a great complement to Rio rather than to continue some sort of insane competition between the cities.

At the end of the day it is satisfying that Brazil has these two major cities: it adds an extra vibrancy to the country. São Paulo and Rio work for Brazil like Los Angeles and New York for the US, Sydney and Melbourne for Australia and Madrid and Barcelona for Spain. I've learnt to accept that Rio is our very own postcard. And if the first things that come to mind for foreigners when they think of Brazil are Christ the Redeemer and hot, bronzed bodies on Ipanema Beach – well, perhaps that is actually not such a bad thing.

In a way, Rio belongs to all Brazilians: everything that happens there will inevitably have an impact on our international image as a country. And besides, whatever Paulistanos say, we will always enjoy spending our weekends in Rio and, yes, we will even do our business there.

In a way, Rio has everything that a Paulistano would like to have. We would certainly swap the treadmills in trendy gym clubs to go for a run on the *calçadão* (promenade). Instead of a cold-pressed juice, we would love to drink our coconut water from a real coconut while watching the sunset at Arpoador. We would delight

Where Rio beats São Paulo

01 Outdoor sports
Who wouldn't prefer a beach run to a treadmill?
02 Embraces
Cariocas really don't hold back on their hugs.
03 Casual clothing
Rio does effortless style better than anyone else.

in taking that irresistible listlessness back with us to São Paulo. And we might even trade the harsher sounds of the Paulistano accent for the charming Carioca tones with that lovely soft "R".

Like everyone in the world we also end up idealising life in Rio – perhaps so much so, in fact, that we end up finding defects and being a little bit bitchy about it as well. We complain about the dodgy cab drivers and the searing heat. But although the city certainly does have its share of problems, I have to admit I agree with the Cariocas: they really do have a marvellous city. — (M)

ABOUT THE WRITER: Fernando Augusto Pacheco has been working for Monocle 24 since 2011. Even though he hails from São Paulo, he loves Rio. The heat and the wonderful swimwear are his favourite things about the city.

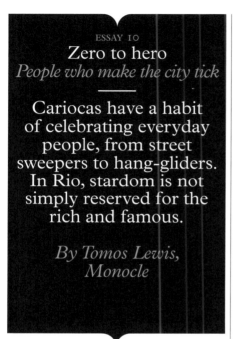

Zero to hero
People who make the city tick

Cariocas have a habit of celebrating everyday people, from street sweepers to hang-gliders. In Rio, stardom is not simply reserved for the rich and famous.

By Tomos Lewis, Monocle

In 1997, as the Rio Carnival entered its final days, the street-cleaner Renato Sorriso began his work sweeping up the glittery detritus of the Carnival floats that had gone before him. The samba music was still playing and the crowd lining the Carnival route was in buoyant mood as the clean-up got underway.

In a swift, spontaneous moment, Sorriso, dressed in the recognisable orange overalls of Rio's municipal rubbish-collectors, launched into a samba routine of his own, using his broom as his dance partner. His frenetic, unscripted performance delighted the crowd. The cheering and the applause intensified as Sorriso's steps became more ambitious, his moves more elaborate.

Hidden within the audience was a camera crew, who had been sent to the Sambadrome to record the colourful, noisy parade that had passed just moments before. Noticing the rising noise from the crowd, they swung their lens in Sorriso's direction and recorded the whole impromptu spectacle. The footage was broadcast later that day and, overnight, Sorriso became a national star. Television talk-shows beckoned, magazine and newspaper columns were penned telling his life story and live performances were arranged in which Gari Sorriso – the Smiling Street Sweeper, as he was nicknamed – reprised his routine to rapturous crowds at music venues right across the city.

So treasured a moment did Sorriso's performance become that the Street Sweepers' Samba has become a permanent fixture on the Carnival calendar: orange-clothed binmen and women strutting their stuff, with brooms in hand, to the music booming around the Sambadrome. Sorriso himself – long cemented as a national treasure in Brazil by the time the

Three city heroes

01 Helô Pinheiro
The woman who inspired the song "The Girl from Ipanema".
02 Madame Sâta
One of the most celebrated drag acts in Brazil.
03 Christ the Redeemer
The most heroic of them all.

"Rio's city heroes don't become so by being revered from afar; these are the people who live and work in the city and make it what it is"

city was awarded the 2016 Olympic Games – had a cameo role in the closing ceremony of London's Olympics.

Sorriso's rise to the pedestal occupied by Rio's city heroes may well read like something of a fairytale. But it says something about the people whom this city reveres and whom it counts among its heroes. In Rio, you are as likely to be celebrated if you are an employee of its rubbish-collection service as you are as the protagonist of the latest telenovela or the superstar striker of Brazil's national football team. This isn't a question of celebrity, although Rio has plenty of those. It isn't the rich and the famous who are truly venerated here: it is the people who say something broader about life in the city itself.

When, in 1991, Rio's favourite sporting son, Pedro Paulo Guise Carneiro Lopes – known simply and affectionately as Pepê – died suddenly whilst competing at the world hang-gliding championships in Tokyo, his home city went into a period of mourning. A cartoon published in a newspaper following his death pictured another of the city's totems, Christ the Redeemer, head bowed, a tear in his eye, cradling Pepê in his upturned palm.

Pepê's place in the hearts of Cariocas may have been sealed by his victory at the hang-gliding world championship of 1981 in Tokyo but he had been a treasure in the city long before that. It is he who popularised surfing in Brazil and, from long days spent at the beach, became one of its most successful beachside entrepreneurs, selling healthy snacks to surfers along the coast, before opening one of Rio's first high-end Japanese restaurants, Sushi Leblon.

Heroic acts, from a civic point of view, are simple ones in Rio de Janeiro – a dancing refuse collector, a naturally skilled footballer who hones his craft on the beach or a young woman walking along a street who inspires a song that comes to define a city ("The Girl from Ipanema"). Rio's city heroes don't become so by being revered from afar; these are the people who live and work in the city and make it what it is. Just like Renato Sorriso who, incidentally, still works as a binman in Rio de Janeiro today. — (M)

ABOUT THE WRITER: Tomos Lewis is MONOCLE's bureau chief in Toronto, formerly a producer at Monocle 24 radio. He previously worked for BBC News in Washington DC, and for the BBC's Welsh-language news services in the UK.

ESSAY 11

The sound of a nation
Brazil's musical creation: samba

To swing your hips to the beat of a samba drum is to understand the rhythm to which the country moves. Rio's, and in fact Brazil's, modern history can be followed through the languid evolution of this sultry song and dance.

By Sheena Rossiter, Monocle

Live samba venues
—
01 Pedra do Sal
Birthplace of 'samba carioca', with an open-air dance floor.
02 Beco do Rato
Simple no-frills bar in the heart of Lapa.
03 Trapiche Gamboa
Large samba club in Gamboa, for dancing till dawn.

There's a reason why one of Rio de Janeiro's nicknames is the City of Samba. From 12-piece samba bands playing on stage at the Municipal Theatre to a cappella songs on the beach with improvised percussion from a glass bottle and a coin, the music can be heard nearly everywhere in Rio.

I remember the first time I actually managed to dance to samba properly. It was miles away from any golden-sand beach in Brazil, or the no-frills, sweaty, concrete samba-school warehouses of Rio's Zona Norte. My samba epiphany happened while dancing around the kitchen table in the house where I grew up back in Edmonton in Alberta, Canada one New Year's Eve. The heating was cranked up, the snow was coming down and we were all bundled up in our ugliest Christmas sweaters as the city experienced its coldest winter in decades.

After having stomped my feet off beat for more than two years in Brazil, I figured I certainly couldn't embarrass myself with my horrendous samba skills on this brief trip home in front of a handful of Canadians. So after a few celebratory New Year's drinks, on came Beth Carvalho's "Vou Festejar" and we were off. Suddenly, as if the magical samba saint had finally come and blessed me with the right rhythm, my hips were shaking and my feet feverishly tapping as Carvalho's raspy and booming voice floated out of the tinny-sounding computer speakers and into the cold Alberta air.

One-two-three. One-two-three. One-two-three.

"You got it! You're doing it!" my sambaholic Brazilian husband cried out joyfully.

I got it? Did this mean no more embarrassing family barbecues? And from that moment on, I too became a sambaholic.

I was so ecstatic about my new-found rhythm that I nearly sambaed off the plane back into my adopted country, ignoring the usual mind-numbing Brazilian bureaucracy and disorganisation that would normally make me immediately tense up upon landing. After all those countless, painful hours waiting in line after line, getting document after document, stamp after stamp, I felt like I was finally reaping the rewards of my Brazilian permanent residency.

Samba originally began as an expression of happiness and a means to forget about suffering. Both the dance and the music date back to times of slavery in the state of Bahia in the northeast of Brazil. The music started when slave masters allowed African slaves, mostly from Angola and Congo, to play instruments from their homelands. The dance was associated with Candomblé, an African religion, and would honour one of the faith's gods.

Now, even though samba can be found throughout Brazil, Rio de Janeiro is known as the cradle of samba. In the late 19th century many freed slaves migrated to Rio de Janeiro from other parts of Brazil and settled in neighbourhoods such as Gamboa in the old port area, earning it the nickname Pequena África (Little Africa). It was here that "samba carioca" truly started, at Pedra do Sal (The Salt Rock). It was originally a meeting place for Candomblé ceremonies but is now a samba venue where live shows are held weekly.

> *"Suddenly, as if the magical samba saint had finally come and blessed me with the right rhythm, my hips were shaking and my feet feverishly tapping"*

The radio era of the 1920s allowed samba to explode into much more than a means of expression for a marginalised group. It started to absorb other parts of Brazilian culture, even making its way onto the football pitch, and began to pique the interest of white middle and upper-class Brazilians. That's when samba really found its identity.

Today there are many different variations of samba. Samba-*canção*:
sentimental samba. Samba *de breque*: dramatic masculine samba. Samba-*enredo*: samba performed by samba schools for the annual Carnival parade. Bossa nova: a fusion of samba and jazz. That's just to name a few.

Alongside this musical evolution came a long list of some world-class musicians: Noel Rosa, Carmen Miranda (the "Brazilian bombshell" who would go on to Hollywood stardom in the 1940s), Martinho da Vila, Paulinho da Viola, Cartola, Elza Soares, Tom Jobim, Vinícius de Moraes, Gilberto Gil, Chico Buarque... the list goes on and on.

Most of these sambistas nurtured their talent in Rio de Janeiro and the epicentre of this samba mecca is the neighbourhood of Lapa. Rows upon rows of bars line the streets, playing live samba music. Over the past few years, since arriving back in Brazil after my so-called samba epiphany, I've wandered through Lapa and I too have evolved since that fateful night. Now, sometimes, I find myself singing along with the other Brazilian sambaholics at a simple samba street bar.

For me, the moment I got samba was really the moment I started to get Brazil. Samba is more than just music: it's a way of life. And the samba way of life, well, that's Brazil. — (M)

ABOUT THE WRITER: Sheena Rossiter is MONOCLE'S correspondent in Rio de Janeiro, and the co-owner and creative director of Dona Ana Films & Multimedia. Her advice for anyone trying to learn how to dance samba: "Don't be overwhelmed by all the different drums. Just pick one drum and dance to it in steps of three."

The muscle show
Rio's fitness obsession

———

Sporting fervour existed long before Fifa and the IOC declared the city as gracious host. Every Carioca is a professional athlete, or at least dresses like one. If you want to join the image-obsessed denizens of Rio, you'll first need to know how to look the part.

By Saul Taylor, Monocle

For such a relaxed city, there's a lot of sweating going on. I say "sweating" but "gleaming" is probably a better description because Cariocas don't sweat: they glaze and glimmer in the heat of the sun. While their Anglo-Saxon compatriots stand motionless in the afternoon shadows willing themselves not to think, fearing even a single thought might trigger the Iguaçu Falls beneath their shirt, the Carioca breezes by in an endless parade of technical fabrics.

Rio might just be the most athletic alfresco place on Earth. Cariocas are sporty by nature: running, cycling and swimming are routine; muscle flexes, energetic embraces and dramatic hair flicks are standard punctuation in conversation. This city –

engraved into the mountains and corralled by the sea – was born from adventure and built for activity. Humans have been beating its paths, swimming its waters and climbing its peaks for centuries. Its climate is conducive (most of the time) to outdoor activity and sport has evolved within the urban landscape. Outdoor gyms appear everywhere and for everyone: for all shapes, shades and sizes; for old people; for kids; for dogs. There are cycle lanes and skate parks; courts, tracks and sandpits; pitches, fields and courses; and trails, paths and waterways covering the entire tropical expanse.

An Olympic spirit existed long before the IOC landed with its measuring tape and stopwatches. Every day in Rio is a day at the Games. Step out onto the pavement and not 20 seconds passes before a jogger bundles by or a cyclist whirrs past. Venture a few steps further and after dodging more runners and bikers, outdoor facilities abound where nimble Cariocas practice football, tennis and table tennis, beach volleyball, rowing, canoeing, basketball, athletics, weightlifting, sailing, trampolining and, er, shooting. Each athlete an amateur in their field but a professional poser at the top of their game.

For an instant immersion into the scene, head down to Ipanema on a Sunday when the municipal guard closes the traffic lanes closest to the beach and a multi-layered slice of Carioca life swoops upon the *calçadão* (promenade). In a city divided by wealth, the beach is the only place where people feel equal; everyone seems the same in a swimsuit. Spry little old ladies outpace the

Best places for a workout

———

01 Dois Irmãos
Hike up the 'Two Brothers' for the best overview of the city.
02 Lagoa
A morning run is a spectacular way to start the day.
03 Ipanema Beach
You name the activity, and you'll find it here.

Muscle Marias on the jogging track, girls on wheels not only turn heads but elicit entire 180-degree body swerves, dogs pull lazy owners on longboards and lifeguards sit surveying the surf from their *postos* on high.

The sand is alive with lithe young things enrapt in "Carioca sports". And although they technically didn't invent them (as they might claim), the denizens of Rio have certainly perfected them. *Altinha* and *frescobol*, keepy-uppy and bat 'n' ball respectively; slackline, the sporting equivalent of a cross-legged hippie playing the Hang; paddle-boarding, a harder-than-it-looks slow surf; and *futevolei*, a form of volleyball played with the feet. All are performed with elegance and grace by everybody.

But beware. Unless you're wearing the right uniform then there is no chance of fitting in with this fitness thing. For the sportsmen the get-up is very simple; mismatched T-shirt or vest and long shorts with a *sunga* (Brazilian Speedo) underneath in preparation for a post-workout swim in the ocean. And post-post-workout swim, the general idea is to allow the sun to dry you off in a standing position, looking as nonchalant as possible. The less it looks like you give a hoot the better.

Beyond the impossibly tight bulges in the hind quarters and the Pelé-thick thighs, distinguishing between the dedicated female gym-goer and the twice-a-weeker is a sport in itself. Firstly, the journey to and from the gym is equally as important as the workout because that's where you get the most looks. Girls who mean business walk the city in yoga pants, sports bra, crop top and neon trainers, accessorised with a heavily caked-on glare that could freeze the Atlantic. The most

"Beyond the impossibly tight bulges in the hind quarters and the Pelé-thick thighs, distinguishing between the dedicated female gym-goer and the twice-a-weeker is a sport in itself"

obvious tell, however, is the socks. Known as the *meião* or "long-sock" look, they wear knee-high footballers' socks to protect their calves during a particular exercise that tightens their arse by strapping weights to their shins. The pursuit of perfection is clearly a Carioca obsession.

While LA might have invented the modern-day gym and counts Santa Monica in its alfresco arsenal, its lack of respect for the pedestrian strikes it from true outdoor-city status. Sydney may boast beaches from Bondi to Balmoral but come winter we dare anyone but the hardiest Sydneysider to swim in the surf. Rio's charm lies in its jogability and year-round sun but its most attractive trait is the Cariocas themselves in their equal dedication to sport and the aesthetics of developing technique. And that, in a single thrust, is the essential salt that all the sweat boils down to: it's not only the final result that counts, it's also how good you look achieving it. — (M)

ABOUT THE WRITER: Saul Taylor was one of the founding editors of MONOCLE and, after heading up the Mayor of Rio's international communications team, has returned to what he does best: drinking, dancing and occasionally exercising in the name of editorial excellence – and all still in Rio.

Culture
── A guide
to the arts

The Marvellous City has long been considered the cultural capital of Brazil and although São Paulo snaps at its arty heels, Rio is still the birthplace of samba and bossa nova, the global Carnival queen and by far the most important centre for the country's television and film industries. With annual art and film festivals that have begun to attract attention from heavyweight international collectors and producers, Brazil's creative community is also favouring Rio as the place to lay down roots.

As the massive port zone rejuvenation takes shape, the city's artists, film-makers and musicians are opening ateliers and studios. This project is promising to make Rio a true creative contender on an international scale. Throw in the largest and wildest Carnival celebration in the world, a tidy list of live venues and a constant stream of museums and galleries popping up across town and Rio feels like it's finally making a business of what it does best: entertainment and spectacle.

Museums and galleries
Must-see collections

①
Museu de Arte do Rio, Centro
Flying the flag

The first of the promised Olympic legacy developments to launch in the revitalised port zone, the Museu de Arte do Rio is spread between an old and new building in the freshly inaugurated Praça Mauá square opposite the Museum of Tomorrow.

With a bias towards Carioca and Brazilian art and culture, the museum's permanent Projeto Morrinho sculpture of a favela by Cirlan de Oliveira alone draws crowds who peer through the glass to get a glimpse. The rooftop restaurant Mauá offers an interesting take on Brazilian cuisine and overlooks the entire port zone; it's a recommended tasty spot for lunch during the week.
Praça Mauá, 5
+ 55 (21) 3031 2741
museudeartedorio.org.br

Unified in motion
─
Inspired by a wave, the undulating roof of the museum was an idea dreamed up by architectural practice Bernardes + Jacobsen Arquitetura as a way to link three buildings of differing architectural styles: Palacete Dom João, the former police building and Rio's old central bus station.

②
Mac de Niterói, Boa Viagem
Stellar design

Cariocas say that the only reason
to visit Niterói – their sister city
across the bay – is to admire Rio
from the other side. But there is
one more thing to behold: the
Oscar Niemeyer-designed Mac
(Museum of Contemporary Art).
Visitors come here to pose
for pictures with the "upturned
spaceship". Take the ferry – or
cross the 14km-long bridge that
was built in the 1970s – to marvel
at the masterpiece. A nice option
is to spend the rest of the day
at Itacoatiara Beach a few
kilometres south.
Mirante da Boa Viagem,
+ 55 (21) 2620 2400
macniteroi.com.br

❸
Centro Cultural Banco do Brasil,
Centro
Big-ticket exhibitions

When the Picasso exhibition
arrived here in 2015 the queues
snaked around the building for
weeks. Set in the original Banco
do Brasil building that was
opened in 1906, the exhibition
space has included a cinema,
theatre and live-music venue
since it opened as a museum
in the late 1980s. When the big
travelling exhibitions such as
MC Escher, Yayoi Kusama and
Kandinsky come to Brazil they
often make the CCBB the first
stop on the tour.
Rua Primeiro de Março, 66
+ 55 (21) 3808 2020
culturabancodobrasil.com.br

④
Museu do Amanhã, Centro
The tomorrow people

The sustainable paint is barely
dry on Rio's newest, shiniest and
greenest museum. Designed by
every town planner's favourite
architect Santiago Calatrava,
the "Museum of Tomorrow"
was created to explore the
impact of issues such as climate
change, population growth,
global integration and diversity.
Visitors are encouraged to project
themselves and their children
50 years into the future. The
museum's exoskeleton includes
solar panels that move as the
sun crosses the sky to maximise
their intake of energy.
Praça Mauá, 1
museudoamanha.org.br

Future forecast
Find out what tomorrow will bring

⑤
Sítio Roberto Burle Marx,
Barra de Guaratiba
Modernist's backyard

This 35-hectare estate located just within the city limits used to be the home of Roberto Burle Marx, Brazil's most famous modernist landscape artist, who was responsible for collaborations with Niemeyer and the Copacabana "Portuguese-stone" mosaic pavements. It is necessary to make an appointment but the hassle of booking and making the journey are forgotten after a stroll through the lushly haphazard grounds. Combine it with lunch at Bira de Guaratiba (*see page 30*) just a couple of kilometres away.
Estrada Roberto Burle Marx, 2019
+55 (21) 2410 1412
sitioburlemarx.blogspot.com.br

Hip to be square

Pedestrianised square Praça Mauá is the star of the 5 million sq m port zone redevelopment that includes the Mar, Museu do Amanhã and a plucky new VLT tram that links to the rest of the transport system.

⑥
Museu de Arte Moderna, Flamengo
Concrete bastion

Architect Affonso Reidy's Mam was inaugurated in 1948 back when a brutal bit of modernism felt like the future. It might look a little worn around its concrete edges these days but it still manages to woo the best in contemporary art.

Recent exhibitions have profiled Ron Mueck, Damián Ortega and photographer João Pina. An exit through the gift shop is highly recommended: besides postcards and pencil sharpeners you can also pick up original pieces of furniture by Sérgio Rodrigues and his friends.
Avenida Infante Dom Henrique, 85
+ 55 (21) 2240 4944
mamrio.org.br

Keeping it natural
———
Mam is located in Rio's largest urban park (called Aterro do Flamengo). The story of the reclaimed land plot and its modernist designer Lota de Macedo Soares is told in the 2013 film "Reaching for the Moon".

⑦
Instituto Moreira Salles, Gávea
Brazilian focus

Another of Brazil's cultural
heavyweights, philanthropist
Walther Moreira Salles (father
of film-makers Walter and João
Moreira Salles's) founded this
institute to focus on Brazilian
arts development and promote
cultural programming. The visitor
centre opened in the family home
in Gávea in 1999 just before
Walther's death in 2001. Arthouse
and documentary films are shown
in the cinema most afternoons and
there is also an exhibition space,
café and a shop to buy books
about Brazilian film and art.
*Rua Marquês de São Vicente, 476
+55 (21) 3284 7400
ims.com.br*

Commercial galleries
The exhibitionists

①
Lurixs, Botafogo
Geometry lessons

Botafogo has recently risen as
a neighbourhood for young artists
and creatives to live and set up
shop but Lurixs has long enjoyed
the charm of this residential quarter
having opened back in 2002. Bold
graphic artists such as Elizabeth
Jobim and Luciano Figueiredo form
the stable's style and Lurixs artists
have also found their way into the
permanent collections at Moma
in New York and London's Tate
Modern. While you're in the 'hood
grab lunch at IrajáGastro or Oui
Oui on Rua Conde de Irajá.
*Rua Paulo Barreto, 77
+55 (21) 2541 4935
lurixs.com*

②
Rio Arts Club, Gávea
Visionaries' meeting place

The Rio Arts Club is an arts
social club and co-working
space founded by Frenchman
Sacha Gielbaum, who landed
in Rio in 2009. Located in
a detached house in Gávea,
an area that has become popular
with a more sophisticated arts
crowd, the club is a cool spot
to meet Rio's artistic types.
All manner of trendy young
things from sculptors to graphic
designers can be found relaxing
or working in *casa*, which has
six rooms that are given or
rented out to visiting artists.
*Rua Mary Pessoa, 116
+55 (21) 3489 5986*

Artur Fidalgo, Copacabana
Art superstore

Artur Fidalgo's location in Shopping
Cidade Copacabana is almost as
interesting as the immersive list of
artists that he represents. The mall
was designed by Henrique Mindlin
in the 1960s and is a sweeping warren
of mid-century furniture shops on
the upper floors and an odd mix of
hardware stores and clothes outlets on
the ground level.

Fidalgo's gallery is open every
weekday and hosts revolving
exhibitions from the likes of Ernesto
Neto and Bill Lundberg. The space
was expanded in 2005 to allow for
a larger range of artists.
Rua Siqueira Campos, 143
+55 (21) 2549 6278
arturfidalgo.com.br

④
Marsiaj Tempo Galeria, Ipanema
Art by the beach

Before the artistic axis began to
shift towards Botafogo and further
downtown to Centro, Ipanema was
the gallery capital of the city. This
space has become part of the fabric of
the neighbourhood with a prime spot
just one block away from the sand.

Well-heeled locals often pop in
on their way home from the beach
to speak to owner Laura Marsiaj
or size up a piece for their second
home in Araras in rural Rio State.
Since 2000, Marsiaj has built up
a thick Rolodex of artists that
includes Mariana Mattos, Fabio
Miguez and Rafael Zavagli.
Rua Teixeira de Melo, 31C
+55 (21) 2513 2074
marsiajtempo.com.br

Branching out

Working from his
open-air studio under
a tree in the centre of
Santa Teresa, artist Gétulio
Damado sells incredible
naive sculptures made
from everyday ephemera
for as little as R$20.

③
A Gentil Carioca, Centro
Protest vote

Founded by three artists in 2003,
A Gentil Carioca has become a
reference for quality political and
activist art in Brazil. The team
regularly installs sculptures on the
exterior of the gallery and builds
street furniture for people to sit
on and enjoy.
Rua Gonçalves Lêdo, 11
+55 (21) 2222 1651
agentilcarioca.com.br

The space
—
The gallery was designed by Guilherme Wisnik

I like the feathered brushwork on this piece

⑥
Silvia Cintra + Box 4, Gávea
Family reunion

Something of a local institution herself with more than 20 years' experience on the contemporary art scene, Silvia Cintra moved to her stylish gallery in Gávea in 2010 to merge with her daughter Juliana's Box 4 Gallery. The duo now concentrate on raising the profile of both established and up-and-coming artists. Keep an eye out for Amilcar de Castro and Marilá Dardot.
Rua das Acácias, 104
+ 55 (21) 2521 0426
silviacintra.com.br

⑦
Galeria Nara Roesler, Ipanema
Leading Brazilian talents

Slap bang in the heart of Ipanema between the beach and the picturesque Lagoa lagoon, this perfectly proportioned converted house played host to Vik Muniz's acclaimed *Album* show during the city's annual ArtRio commercial-art fair. Muniz could be found lolling on the wall outside enjoying a cocktail and joking with passers-by or giving anyone who asked politely a free dissection of the work inside. Other artists on the roster include Xavier Veilhan, Antonio Dias and Abraham Palatnik.
Rua Redentor, 241
+55 (21) 3591 0052
nararoesler.com.br

Changing lives through art
———
In 2014 Vik Muniz opened his Vidigal School NGO within the eponymous favela in association with MIT. The aim is to educate artistic but disadvantaged kids from all over the city and help integrate social classes through art.

⑧
Galeria 1500 Babilônia, Leme
New beginnings

Galeria 1500 was one of the first
galleries to open in a favela. The
Morro da Babilônia community is
situated above Leme, a leafy and
oft-forgotten neighbourhood at the
north end of Copacabana.

Galeria 1500 originated in New
York but moved to Rio with its
founder Alex Bueno de Moraes in
2014. Specialising in photography,
the gallery represents artists such
as Bruno Cals, Beatriz Franco and
Hirosuke Kitamura. It is well worth
a wander into the community for a
slice of actual favela life and a chance
to see some real local talent.
Rua Marquês de Abrantes, 19
+55 (21) 3827 3727
1500babilonia.com

I call this
one 'Rio in
the present'

⑨
Anita Schwartz Galeria de
Arte, Gávea
Talent spotter

Schwartz has been active on the
Carioca art scene for more than
30 years. Her chic 700 sq m space
is located just steps from Baixo
Gávea, a tiny neighbourhood where
the city's young things congregate
from Thursday to Sunday to flirt
and drink in the square and grab
a bite at Braseiro da Gávea (*see
page 40*). Schwartz is responsible
for fostering local and international
visual artists including Otavio
Schipper, Nuno Ramos and
Luis Coquenão.
*Rua José Roberto Macedo
Soares, 30*
+55 (21) 2274 3873
anitaschwartz.com.br

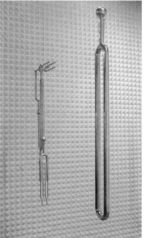

Sweet set-up
—
Artists now use this former chocolate factory

⑩
Fábrica Bhering, Santo Cristo
Selection box

At 16,000 sq m the former Fábrica Bhering chocolate factory is a giant hive of creativity. With more than 80 painters, photographers, sculptors, artisans and small businesses having set up their studio spaces inside the building, Bhering has become the axis around which the port zone grows its independent creative credentials.

On weekdays visitors can cast their eye over Rio's emerging talent and bag a future Vik Muniz or Campana Brothers for a steal. Artists and artisans include Adoro Adorno, Atelier do Terraço and Lucio Volpini.
Rua Orestes, 28
+55 (21) 2213 0014
fabricabhering.com

Carnival
The rhythm of Rio

①
Carnival
Time to celebrate

Rio's version of this euphoric worldwide event is without doubt the biggest and most famous of them all. While its roots are in Catholicism, it's the time when Cariocas get to flaunt their fun-loving personalities with plenty of feathers, floats, glitter and exposed skin.

The official samba parades that take place in the Sambadrome mobilise fans and supporters much like a football match. Different samba schools associated with various neighbourhoods – most from Rio's less-affluent areas – compete and are judged in categories including harmony, percussion, song and costume.

Do not mistake fun-loving with chaos however: these parades are highly organised and orchestrated. Tickets to see them go from R$20 up to R$1,000 depending on seating sector but another way to join in on the fun is by parading yourself: all the schools sell costumes online and you can register up until December.
rio-carnival.net

I'm not sure if this is supposed to go on my head or my bum

How to do Carnival

Whether you've got tickets to see the official parades in the Sambadrome or not, there are plenty of ways to enjoy the festivities. Carnival is the most cherished holiday in Brazil and although it officially only lasts three days, the revelry starts a month before and ends beyond it too. If you are visiting during the period, find one of the city's *blocos de rua* or street blocks, where thousands dance along behind the floats playing roaring samba music and *batucada* (booming percussion). You can't miss these parades. Streets are closed off in several parts of the city and the atmosphere is electric. Although there are new additions every year, here are our top picks for *blocos de rua*.

01 Céu na Terra, Santa Teresa: This *bloco*, the name of which translates to "heaven on Earth", parades through the cobbled streets of the neighbourhood and attracts a large and friendly crowd.

02 Suvaco do Cristo, Jardim Botânico: The name translates to "Armpit of Christ", alluding to the district directly under Christ the Redeemer's right arm.

03 Banda de Ipanema, Ipanema: Founded during the military dictatorship in 1964, this *bloco* attracts people of all ages and backgrounds. It once counted on the faithful presence of Oscar Niemeyer and singer Chico Buarque.

Cinemas
The best seats in town

①
Centro Cultural Luiz Severiano
Ribeiro – Cine Odeon, Centro
Sepia tones

Rio has a longstanding cinematic
history and remains the capital of
Brazil's film industry. The annual
Festival do Rio draws international
film-makers in October and one of
the key venues is the Cine Odeon.
After a recent renovation it is
back in the hands of its original
owner Grupo Severiano Ribeiro,
the founder of which brought
movies to Brazil in 1916: he opened
the Odeon in the now-famous
downtown neighbourhood of
Cinelândia (Cinemaland).
Praça Floriano, 7
+55 (21) 2461 0201
kinoplex.com.br

Rolling in Rio

RioFilme and the Rio Film
Commission were set up
to leverage Rio's varied
landscapes and advanced
audiovisual infrastructure.
The city currently outplays the
rest of the country with about
60 per cent of productions
being made here in recent
years.

Rio on film

01 Cidade de Deus, 2002:
This film, set between the
1960s and 1980s in the
City of God favela, was
released in 2002. It was
eventually nominated in
2004 for four Academy
Awards, including best
director (Fernando
Meirelles) and best
adapted screenplay.
02 Rio, 2011: Carioca
animator Carlos
Saldanha's colourful
love letter to his own
hometown, this charming
depiction of birdlife
in Brazil and its 2014
follow-up *Rio 2* is a must
for any inbound flight
to the Marvellous City.
03 Waste Land, 2010:
Documentary following
Brazil's most famous
living artist Vik Muniz,
as he plans and executes
one of his most ambitious
and heart-rending
artworks with the
litter-pickers of the
now-defunct Jardim
Gramacho landfill site.

②
Casa de Cultura Laura Alvim,
Ipanema
Beach scene

Laura Alvim turned her family
home into an eponymous cultural
centre after the death of her
father Álvaro Alvim (who
introduced the x-ray to Brazil).
Considered by some to be the
first "girl from Ipanema",
Alvim dedicated her life to
film, theatre and art after her
family prevented her from
becoming an actress.
    While Alvim passed away
in 1984, her open-house policy
continued as she donated her
property with its three cinema
screens, museum, gallery space
and room for theatre productions
to the government. Sitting on one
of the most sought-after stretches of
beach in Rio, the property is a
slither of cultural enlightenment
on "millionaires' row".
Avenida Vieira Souto, 176
+55 (21) 2332 2016
*cultura.rj.gov.br/espaco/casa
-de-cultura-laura-alvim*

Music venues
Soul of the city

③
Bip Bip, Copacabana
Samba central

Turn into Rua Almirante
Gonçalves after 21.00 on most
nights and you can't miss Bip
Bip. Patrons flow out into the
residential street from this tiny
bar, craning their necks to see
some of Rio's most famous
musicians such as Paulinho
da Viola and Zé Renato &
Geraldo Azevedo. Some say
that Bip Bip is the best place
in the city to see and hear
samba or *choro* – played how
it's meant to be played: among
friends. It's certainly one of the
most authentic live music
experiences you'll have.
Rua Almirante Gonçalves, 50
+ 55 (21) 2267 9696

They'll
love my
drumming
at Pedra
do Sal

④
Circo Voador, Lapa
Alfresco sounds

Most weeknights and every
weekend Circo Voador opens
its doors to the music-obsessed.
Local and international bands
enjoy the rapture of the audience
in this intimate open-air venue
under the famous Lapa arches,
with trams passing overhead. On
Fridays and Saturdays the queue
for the venue cuts chaotically
through the regular Lapa throng
who are drinking beer and dancing
in the street. For Rio first-timers
and those who enjoy spontaneous
parties and high-energy street
life, Circo Voador is a must.
Rua Arcos
+ 55 (21) 2533 0354
circovoador.com.br

①
Pedra do Sal, Saúde
Where it all began

To see samba played on the spot
where most agree it was developed
as a music form, make a beeline
for Pedra do Sal, a simple set of
steps carved into the solid rock face
in a still-gritty corner of the port
zone. This is where salt was traded
(hence the name) and was also the
point where slaves were unloaded
in the 18th and 19th centuries. It
became a residential area for the
black community in Rio, including
those from Bahia in the north of
Brazil. Today the rock doubles
as a perch for samba enthusiasts
who watch and dance to their
favourite acts, especially on
Friday and Monday nights.
Rua Argemiro Bulcão, 1

②
Carioca da Gema, Centro
Hot stuff

Translating as "Carioca gem",
this is one of the city's most
respected music venues. Expect
an agreeably raucous evening
of heavy beats and inevitable
failure when testing out one's
samba steps.
Avenida Mem de Sá, 79
+ 55 (21) 2221 0043
barcariocadagema.com.br

(6)
Beco das Garrafas, Copacabana
And relax...

Just steps from the Belmond
Copacabana Palace and equal in
iconic stature, Beco das Garrafas
is the place to head when your ears
and feet refuse to endure another
samba beat. Since opening in 1960
just after the birth of bossa nova,
every big Brazilian singer, strummer
and stick-man has passed through
this temple to easy listening. If
you're lucky you'll turn up on
a night that Sérgio Mendes, singer
of "Mas Que Nada" – Brazil's
unofficial national anthem – and
Alaíde Costa decide to sing an
impromptu duet.
Rua Duvivier, 37
+55 (21) 2543 2962
becodasgarrafas.mus.br

(5)
Clube dos Democráticos, Centro
Party time

Founded in 1867 as a Carnival
society uniting musicians, dancers
and revellers, this institution has
retained its festive atmosphere. With
a varied programme of live music
from Wednesday through Saturday
it's one of the best places in Rio to
listen to samba classics and dance the
night away. You'll see Cariocas of all
ages sitting and sharing a few beers
while others join the shimmying
masses on the vast dance floor. It's
worth visiting on a Wednesday night
for the weekly Forró session, which
serves as a great introduction to the
music of Brazil's northeast.
Rua do Riachuelo, 91
+55 (21) 2252 1324
clubedosdemocraticos.com.br

I'm wearing
my thong
too!

Radio setlist

01 Mec, 99.3: Something of an institution, Radio Mec (Music, Education and Culture) is the evolution of Brazil's first radio channel Rádio Sociedade. Mec is a high-brow listen and features classical music broadcasting live from the city's top musical events.

02 CBN, 92.5: "The radio that plays news" is the slogan for this Globo-owned news channel that counts 200 reporters, producers, editors, anchors and commentators in its stable. Founded in 1991, CBN has spread from Rio to all major cities with four stations and 32 affiliates across the country. The station is respected for its unbiased news gathering and hard-nosed critical analysis.

03 MPB, 90.3: This station is proud of its claim to be the only one to exclusively play Brazilian music. Its Festival Faro project presents all-new acts to the public; hear styles unique to Brazil, including samba, chorro, funk and forró.

Monocle 24

①
Passion in print
Magazines and newspapers, citywide
From unshakable titles rapidly approaching their second century to considered newcomers reaching niche readers, newsstands in Brazil offer a wealth of choice. Admittedly you'll have to wade through perfectly sculpted abs and gossiping glossies to find the lesser-known titles but beneath those bronzed, glistening bods awaits a worthy stack.

Cool, calm and widely collected Brazilian design magazine ❶ *Bamboo* covers the best in architecture and art.❷ *Véja Rio* is a weekly round-up of the city's social calendar – a reliable resource to help navigate the cultural landscape. The quick-witted and often controversial voice of ❸ *TPM* was born out of frustration over the lack of intelligent reading for women. Attitude-laden articles are lightened by a sprinkling of eye-candy. If Veja Rio is your friendly guide then ❹ *Veja* is the feisty older sister. This current-affairs weekly is incredibly influential but is best read with a healthy pinch of salt. To keep abreast of the business world's wheeling and dealing pick up a copy of the Globo supplement ❺ *Economia*. Or for a newsier broadsheet both ❻ *Folha de S Paulo* and ❼ *O Globo* are seasoned players (the latter is sister company to the broadcasting behemoth Globo). Stemmed from its Parisian counterpart ❽ *Le Monde Diplomatique Brasil* is a monthly affairs magazine with a Brazilian take on the world. And last but by no means least, ❾ *Piauí*'s eloquent long-form writing makes it the closest thing Brazil has to *The New Yorker*.

②
Kiosks, citywide
The rack pack

Rio has a strong kiosk culture; you'll be continually passing these squat boxes packed with global magazines and newspapers. The selection will be much the same in each one: a decent offering of international titles plus cheaper ones for the domestic market. For knowledgeable service our pick is Jose Carlos Novello's newsstand on the corner of Rua Dias Ferreira and Rua General Artigas in Leblon.

Design and architecture
—— Rio in shape and form

Few cities have married themselves to the landscape quite like Rio de Janeiro. Its architects and designers have been inspired – and challenged – by its undulating tropical topography since the city was founded in 1565.

From the quiet grandeur of colonial townhouses to the florid neoclassical revival in the 20th century, Rio's identity as a built environment is an eclectic one. The concrete modernist movement that characterised Brazilian cities from the 1960s has its flourishes here, and the giants of Brazilian architecture – Oscar Niemeyer, Roberto Burle Marx and Lucio Costa – have left their mark too.

At the same time, the middle of the 20th century was an incredibly rich period for Brazilian design with figures such as Sérgio Rodrigues, Joaquim Tenreiro and Ricardo Fasanello putting Rio firmly on the map. This heritage is still visible in the city today, from the bijou furniture shops on Rua Lavradio to the larger-scale architectural projects around the city.

Modern architecture
Sign of the times

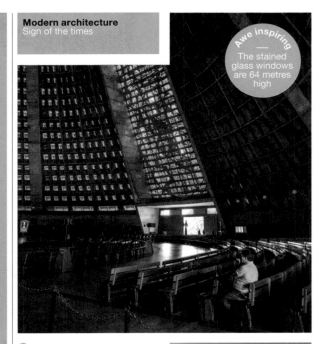

Awe inspiring
The stained glass windows are 64 metres high

1

Catedral Metropolitana de São Sebastião, Centro
Sublime interpretation

Rio's imposing conical cathedral is a marvel of religious architecture and a late addition to the city's concrete revolution. Inspired loosely by Mayan pyramids, it was designed by Edgar Oliveira da Fonseca and consecrated in 1979 during the military dictatorship. It therefore holds a somewhat contested place in the hearts of many of the faithful in Rio. Nevertheless, it is difficult not to be awed when walking into its vast circular interior: four floor-to-ceiling stained-glass panels (each 64 metres tall) meet at the cathedral's apex to form the shape of a crucifix.

The cathedral has a small, colourful museum of religious relics, including the personal effects of Cardinal Jaime de Barros Câmara, the archbishop of Rio de Janeiro between 1943 and 1971.
Avenida República do Chile, 245
+55 (21) 2240 2669
catedral.com.br

Why am I trying to reach the apex using balloons?

② Museu de Arte Moderna, Flamengo
Creative community

Affonso Eduardo Reidy's cathedral to Brazilian contemporary art comes to life at dusk. Soon-to-be-married couples practise their first dances here, skateboarders wheel beneath the building and musicians strum away.

The museum was completed in 1955 on reclaimed land and is surrounded by the modernist public gardens of landscape architect Roberto Burle Marx. The concrete supports (shaped like flat, stylised spiders' legs) are outside, freeing up the space within and creating largely uninterrupted sea views.
Avenida Infante Dom Henrique, 85
+ 55 (21) 3883 5600
mamrio.com.br

Petrol stations

The neo-concrete movement in Brazil has left some very unsubtle marks on Rio de Janeiro's landscape. A good example of this is in the form of two petrol stations on either side of Lagoa. They're intriguing interpretations of the design style that came to characterise much of Brazilian urban architecture from 1959 onwards.

On the northeastern lip of the lagoon is a squat, single-span concrete dome between the pumps – a modernist pavilion in miniature. To the south, a white gazebo made of strips of interlocking concrete and embossed with soft-angled stylised designs forms a rather classy canopy beneath which to refill your car.

③ Central do Brasil Station, Centro
First class

This station, first established in 1858, now only operates regional trains. Back in the day it was an important landmark of Rio de Janeiro's socioeconomic development during Portuguese rule. The original building was demolished in 1939; the current structure had its imposing clock tower inaugurated in 1943 during the Estado Novo authoritarian regime. Modernist buildings created during this period were held up as markers of Brazil's progress. The 135-metre-high geometric and aerodynamic tower is a striking example of Rio's art deco architecture.
Praça Cristiano Ottoni

Pieced together
———
An important contributor to the modernist movement in Brazil, Paulo Werneck is often credited with bringing mosaics to the country. His works can be seen on residential walls throughout and on architectural feats, such as the Niemeyer-designed Banco Boavista HQ.

④ Costa Brava Clube, Joatinga
Sailing ahead

Built in 1962 by brothers Ricardo and Renato Menescal, this modernist club could double as the headquarters of a classic Bond villain. The complex engineering feat resembles a ship at sea and sits at the tip of Joatinga Beach with views out on the ocean and the Dois Irmãos and Pedra da Gávea mountains.

The Menescal brothers were important practitioners in Rio, having built other institutions (such as the city's planetarium). The way the building overcomes topographical challenges and its natural elements (such as the salt-water pool) are significant features of modern Carioca architecture. Hosting society weddings and New Year's Eve parties in its heyday, the club is now slightly worn around the edges – but this also adds to its faded grandeur.
Endereço Clube, Rua Sargento José da Silva, 3621
+ 55 (21) 3139 1850
costabravaclube.com.br

Talent pool
—
Three leading architects were on the team

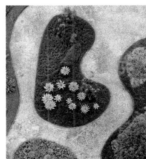

⑤

Edifício Gustavo Capanema, Centro
Starchitect collaboration

This is one of the earliest and finest
examples of modernist architecture
in Rio. The former headquarters
of the Ministry of Education and
Culture, named after the author and
pedagogue Gustavo Capanema, was
built between 1936 and 1945.

Renowned Brazilian architect
Lucio Costa ran the project. Working
in his practice at the time were two
young guns who would go on to
become internationally esteemed:
Oscar Niemeyer (*see page 109*) and
Affonso Eduardo Reidy.

The building rests on 10-metre-
tall stilts and its 16 storeys are solid
materials: iron, concrete, marble
and glass. There are also Burle
Marx-designed gardens, sculptures
by Bruno Giorgi and Celso Antônio
and mosaics by Candido Portinari
(*see page 110*). Today, along with a
bookshop, the building also houses
a space for exhibitions and events.
Rua da Imprensa, 16
+55 (21) 2240 3344
mapadecultura.rj.gov.br

⑥
Conjunto Habitacional Prefeito
Mendes de Moraes, São Cristóvão
Thoughtful social housing

This 1947 residential complex for
civil servants, nicknamed Pedregulho,
is one of the best examples of
modernist architect Affonso
Eduardo Reidy's social projects
and has clear Niemeyer and Le
Corbusier influences. It encompassed
commercial centres, medical units,
a nursery, sports facilities and a
pool. Noteworthy elements are
the pilotis (which overcame uneven
topography) and the *cobogó*, or
hollow concrete, to control lighting
and airflow. Other highlights are
the tiled panel by Candido Portinari
in the gym and gardens by Roberto
Burle Marx.
Rua Marechal Jardim, 450

⑦
Parque Eduardo Guinle, Laranjeiras
Innovative design

This green space was created in the
early 1900s around businessman
Eduardo Guinle's residence. In 1940,
the park was made public.
　Lining it today are three modernist
apartment blocks designed by Lucio
Costa (called Nova Cintra, Bristol
and Caledônia) and constructed
between 1909 and 1913. What makes
them interesting, aside from their
creator, is that they make extensive
use of *cobogós* (*see left*) modular-screen
façades with a pattern of hollow
segments. Costa was a great admirer
of Le Corbusier and the influence
of the European master is obvious
in this, one of Rio's very first mass-
housing projects.
Rua Gago Coutinho, 66

8
Edifício Biarritz, Flamengo
Stroll through the ages

Walk down Praia do Flamengo, the
boulevard separating the apartments
overlooking Guanabara Bay and
the Aterro do Flamengo, and you'll
pass buildings from all eras, from the
1930s stucco ornamentation at the
corner of Rua Ferreira Viana to
the neoclassicism of the Seabra
Mansion. But the real gem is the
Edifício Biarritz, designed in 1940
by Henri Paul Pierre Sajous and
August Rendu. Its striking features
are the symmetrical semi-circular
balconies with railings covered in
ironwork shells and the block's
entrance, with the name stamped
above in bold art deco type.
Praia do Flamengo, 268
+55 (21) 2552 3949

Oscar Niemeyer
Modern great

①
Sambadrome, Centro
Rio's festive heart

If there is one thing that gets
Cariocas as excited as going to
a football match in the Maracanã
Stadium, it is heading to the
Sambadrome during Carnival.
The famous 700-metre strip
flanked by grandstands was
designed by Oscar Niemeyer and
built in 1984 to host the annual
five-day parade of samba schools.
　The stretch is officially known
as Darcy Ribeiro Runway, named
after the renowned anthropologist,
author and politician who worked
with Niemeyer on the project.
Because of Ribeiro's focus on
social and educational projects,
Niemeyer consolidated classrooms,
nurseries and medical units
around the Sambadrome.
　Apotheosis Square is found at
the end of the runway, with the
Niemeyer concrete parabolic
arch indicating the end point.
If you are visiting during Easter
you can buy tickets for the
spectacle of percussionists,
dancers, musicians, floats and
feathered costumes (*see page 98*)
that has become synonymous
with the city. If possible, try to see
one of the technical rehearsals.
Rua Marquês de Sapucaí
+55 (21) 2976 7310
sambadrome.com

2
Mac de Niterói, Boa Viagem
Out-of-this-world design

You would be forgiven for thinking
a flying saucer is about to land.
This notorious Niemeyer project
was inaugurated in 1996 and is
located in the city of Niterói, across
the Guanabara Bay from Rio.
　The circular top is balanced on
a nine-metre-diameter cylindrical
base with a reflecting pool
underneath, supposedly alluding
to a growing flower. The museum
was built upon Niemeyer's return
from exile during the dictatorship
and is one of the best examples
of the architect's articulation of a
"curved" universe.
Mirante da Boa Viagem
+55 (21) 2620 2400
macniteroi.com.br

③
Banco Boavista HQ, Centro
Modernist marvel

This 1948 building is one of the
finest Niemeyer projects. You only
need to walk through the pilotis
area, intertwined with an undulating
glass-brick façade, to appreciate the
sheer dexterity of his work. Note
also the wooden brise-soleil on
the western side, mosaic by Paulo
Werneck in the mezzanine and the
Candido Portinari screen inside.
Praça Pio X, 118

④
Casa das Canoas, São Conrado
House style

Designed in 1951, Canoas was
used as Niemeyer's family home
until 1965 when the architect
was forced to abandon Brazil
due to pressure from the military
dictatorship.
    The house follows the
core principles of modernist
architecture but every detail has
Niemeyer's personal signature:
curved lines integrate the
construction with the surrounding
vegetation and concrete slabs are
suspended over thin pilotis; there
is a lack of decorative elements
and minimal furnishing.
    The shapes of the roof and
foundation of the house are
abstract, curved and free, while its
transparent-glass walls make the
construction disappear within the
tropical forest around it. Through
this Niemeyer emphasises the
elegance of nature.
Estrada das Canoas, 2310
+ 55 (21) 3322 0642
casadascanoas.com.br

I think I
spy another
Niemeyer
masterpiece

⑤
Hospital Federal da Lagoa,
Jardim Botânico
Social conscience

This 1958 hospital demonstrates how
modernism in Brazil was connected
to notions of modernity itself: concern
for social development and attention
to technological advances were
guiding principles in the development
of public spaces.
    Together with fellow architect
Helio Uchoa and landscape architect
Roberto Burle Marx, Niemeyer
used his V-shaped pilotis here, a
creation that became both famous
and fashionable in other national and
international projects. The glazed
eastern façade guarantees views
over the lagoon.
Rua Jardim Botânico, 501
+ 55 (21) 3111 5108

⑥
Obra do Berço, Lagoa
The start of something

Nieymeyer's first project, and a
significant cornerstone of his career,
Obra do Berço's construction
was between 1937 and 1939 while
he was working in Lucio Costa's
practice. Developed compactly
over pilotis and brise-soleil, the
design follows the core principles
of Le Corbusier to the letter.
    It was built to serve as the
headquarters of a philanthropic
institution for young mothers and
children and home to a crèche.
Niemeyer did not charge for the
project and paid for the installation
of the brise-soleil himself.
Rua Cicero Góis Monteiro, 19
+ 55 (21) 2527 0031
aobradobercorj.org.br

Candido Portinari

One of Brazil's most
celebrated painters was born
to Italian immigrants in the
state of São Paulo in 1903.
He moved to Rio at the age
of 15. After spending some
time in Paris, Portinari began
painting frescoes of Brazilian
social and historic scenes:
a characteristic theme that
would mark his whole oeuvre.
    During the 1940s Portinari
became increasingly active
politically, mixing with the
country's top intellectual
and artistic minds and later
affiliating himself with the
Communist party, a move
that led to his temporary
exile in Uruguay.
    He collaborated with
architect Oscar Niemeyer
and other modernist greats
on several projects both
in Rio and in the newly
established capital Brasilia.
One of his greatest pieces
is found adorning the Banco
Boavista HQ in Rio (*see left*),
designed by Niemeyer. But
undoubtedly his most famous
(and largest) mural, "War and
Peace", now hangs in the UN
headquarters in New York.

Legacy buildings
Journey through history

①
Igreja da Glória, Glória
Colonial charm

This tiny church atop a hill is one of the greatest specimens of colonial architecture in Rio. It was founded in the first half of the 18th century by Lieutenant José Cardoso de Ramalho. The Portuguese royal family took a particular liking to this church and many family members were baptised here.

The wooden ornaments inside mark the transition from the end of the rococo period to the neoclassical period. Also remarkable are the 8,000 Portuguese-style tiles decorating the interior.
*Praça Nossa Senhora da Glória, 26
+ 55 (21) 2225 2869
outeirodagloria.org.br*

②

Real Gabinete Português
de Leitura, Centro
Literary grandeur

The Royal Portuguese Reading
Chamber is tucked away down a
backstreet just off the busy Praça
Tiradentes square between Lapa
and Centro. It is easily missed but
shouldn't be. The neo-Manueline
building was founded in 1888 by
Portuguese migrants who wanted a
repository for the cultural heritage
of their motherland. Portuguese
architect Rafael da Silva e Castro
was given the task of designing a
building fit for this brief.

The neo-gothic exterior is
exquisite but is outdone by the
interior, which features hand-
carved wooden bookshelves,
painted galleries running all
around the chamber, a stained-
glass ceiling and a colossal
wrought-iron chandelier. The
collection is impressive too:
350,000 tomes.
Rua Luís de Camões, 30
+55 (21) 2221 3138
realgabinete.com.br

It takes a
lot of effort
to be this
wise

Maracanã Stadium, Maracanã
Place of worship

In a country that treats football as a religion, Maracanã Stadium is held up as a holy temple. Construction started in 1948 as the main venue to host the 1950 World Cup, a project that ended in bitter ignominy. Reports from the competition speak of more than 200,000 people crammed into unfinished stands.

The stadium was redeveloped for the 2014 World Cup to meet new Fifa standards: the top tier was removed and the capacity lowered to 77,000 spectators. A new roof designed by Daniel Fernandes at Stuttgart-based Schlaich Bergermann & Partner was added, made from curved fibreglass membrane sections suspended between rigid axes.
Avenida Presidente Castelo Branco
+55 (21) 2568 9962
maracana.com

Olympic architecture

When Rio was awarded the Summer Olympics in 2009, the challenge for the would-be architects was clear: how to build within a stunning natural landscape that speaks largely for itself. The winning masterplan came from Aecom (which was responsible for much of London's Olympic architecture in 2012).

The Olympic Park is circled by mountains situated on the lip of the beautiful Lagoa de Jacarepaguá in Barra da Tijuca. The site is a former Formula 1 course (the snaking pathways that link the 15 venues here resemble the curves of the old racetrack). Brazilian architects have been coupled with international firms to build the arenas.

Theatro Municipal, Centro
European influence

This theatre is one of four stately buildings that line the historic Praça Marechal Floriano square (along with the National Library, Museum of Fine Arts and the City Council building) but it is the jewel in the crown. It is one of the best examples of architecture from a period often described as the "Carioca belle epoque", which roughly ran from 1898 to 1914 and was characterised by a European aesthetic and sensibility.

Construction began in 1905 under the supervision of mayor Pereira Passos and the design was by Brazilian engineer Francisco de Oliveira Passos and French architect Albert Guilbert. The pair incorporated numerous materials into the neoclassical structure, from marble and onyx to bronze, hardwoods and mosaics.

Theatro Municipal reopened in 2010 after an extensive restoration that cost R$64m. It's possible to wander round the interior from Tuesday to Saturday.
Praça Floriano
+55 (21) 2332 9191
theatromunicipal.rj.gov.br

④

Ilha Fiscal, Centro
Custom-made history

The customs station on this island in Guanabara Bay was designed by engineer Adolfo del Vecchio and built between 1881 and 1889. It is remarkable for its flamboyant neo-gothic architecture and its place in the history of Rio de Janeiro. It was the venue that emperor Dom Pedro II chose to host the final Imperial Ball, just days before he and his family were forced into exile from Brazil and the republic was declared. The island was connected to the mainland in 1931.
Ilha das Cobras, Guanabara Bay
+55 (21) 2104 6025
rio.rj.gov.br

Launch site

The customs station was a key location in the 1893 Brazilian Naval Revolt, which saw the Navy's admirals protest with force against the unconstitutional government. In 1914 control of the island was handed from the Ministry of Finance to the navy.

①
Christ the Redeemer, Parque
Nacional da Tijuca
Lighting the way

In Italy on 12 October 1931, just
after midnight, shortwave radio
pioneer Guglielmo Marconi flicked
a switch and in Rio de Janeiro
the newly completed statue
of Christ the Redeemer was
illuminated for the first time. Its
crisp white silhouette is now a
glowing figure each night atop
Corvocado Mountain.

Designed by the Brazilian
engineer Heitor da Silva Costa,
artist Carlos Oswald and sculptors
Paul Landowski and Gheorghe
Leonida, the statue is made of
reinforced concrete and is 30 metres
tall. During the design process,
Da Silva Costa was convinced he
was "marching towards inevitable
artistic failure", primarily due to
his dislike of concrete as a building
material because of its rough finish.
He solved the problem by studding
the statue with thousands of tiny,
flat triangular shards of soapstone
processed by volunteers in
the parishes at the foot of the
mountain. They wrote messages
to their loved ones on the back of
the white stones before they were
attached as a mosaic to the body
of the statue.
Parque Nacional da Tijuca
corcovado.com.br

② Jardim Botânico
Green jewel

These botanical gardens were
opened by Dom João IV of Portugal
in 1808, the year the seat of the
Portuguese court was transferred
from Lisbon to Rio de Janeiro.
The original idea was to cultivate
crops from across the Portuguese
empire, particularly spices from the
East Indies, and to research their
attributes. Some of the first plants
to arrive were Imperial Palm trees.
Every tree of this kind in Rio today
– and there are many – allegedly
derives from this first crop.

The gardens are laid out
beautifully with gravel paths,
ponds, pergolas and fountains.
The area outside the multiple
greenhouses holds about 9,000
botanical specimens belonging
to some 1,500 species. Watch out
for the enormous *ceiba pentandra*
from Mexico and the pond's
giant Amazonian water lilies.
Rua Jardim Botânico, 1008
+55 (21) 3874 1808
jbrj.gov.br

③
Parque do Flamengo, Flamengo
Reclaiming the past

The green strip of land running
along the bay from Botafogo
down to Santos Dumont Airport,
popularly known as Aterro do
Flamengo, is a massive piece
of reclaimed land dating back
to the 1950s. At its centre is this
impressive park.

The architectonic elements
of the bank were developed by
Affonso Eduardo Reidy while
Roberto Burle Marx designed
the landscape work. Today the
area contains sports courts
and fields, a cycle path and
footpaths among the diverse
flora of native species.
Near Avenida Infante Dom Henrique

④
Arcos da Lapa, Lapa
Water therapy

The Romanesque double arches of
the Arcos da Lapa (also known as
the Carioca Aqueduct) make up one
of Rio's most striking landmarks. It
was completed in 1723 and its 270-
metre length funnelled water into the
burgeoning city for more than 150
years. In 1896, as Rio modernised
its water-supply infrastructure, it
was transformed into a tramline,
connecting central Rio with the hilly

Santa Teresa neighbourhood. It is
hoped the famous yellow tram cars of
the Bondinho de Santa Teresa will be
up and running again in time for the
Olympic Games.
Near Avenida Mem de Sá

High performance
——
The Arcos da Lapa
was one of the biggest
urban construction projects
of the colonial era. The
aqueduct was overseen by
Brigadier Alpoim, who also
designed the governor's
palace in Ouro
Preto.

⑤
Parque Lage, Jardim Botânico
Rainforest retreat

The grand palatial villa set at the
foot of Corcovado Mountain
represents a collision of historical
majesty and natural beauty. It is
in the middle of this tropical park
and is now home to the city's visual
arts school, having once been the
residence of industrialist Henrique
Lage and his wife, Italian mezzo
soprano Gabriella Besanzoni.
    Under Lage's ownership the
mansion was remodelled by Italian
architect Mario Vodret and the
grounds had a European-style
makeover. But as you venture
further from the house the gardens
meld into the untamed Parque
Nacional da Tijuca. There are
dozens of trails to explore and you
can even hike up Corcovado
Mountain from here. Make sure
you also enter the mansion and
look at the grandiose courtyard
and pool within.
Rua Jardim Botânico, 414
+ 55 (21) 3257 1800
eavparquelage.rj.gov.br

❶
Atelier Ricardo Fasanello,
Santa Teresa
Beauty through function

Born in 1930, Ricardo Fasanello
was one of a raft of mid-century
Brazilian designers who – along
with other leading lights such as
Sérgio Rodrigues and Joaquim
Tenreiro – put the country on the
map for design talent. His furniture
emphasises functionality and comfort
and incorporates curves and spheres;
they are all shapes inspired by his love
of car design. One of his most famous
pieces is the Esfera armchair.
    His old atelier in Santa Teresa
includes a workshop where a small
number of pieces are still made. It's
well worth a visit: some of Fasanello's
most famous pieces sit in a beautiful
little room with a vaulted wooden
ceiling (built by Fasanello himself)
and views over Guanabara Bay.
    Fasanello's widow Olivia
Tarnowski Fasanello and son Ricardo
now open the atelier to the public
by appointment. "For Ricardo
[Senior], design had to be functional
whatever the piece," says Olivia. "The
beauty of it was the last thing he was
interested in. Because if it was
doing what it was meant to do, if
it was functional and comfortable,
then it was naturally beautiful."
Rua do Paraiso, 42
+ 55 (21) 2232 3164
ricardofasanellodesign.com

Fasanello fanclub
———
Philosopher and writer
André Ponce was a great
admirer of Fasanello's
designs. He described the
furniture maker's pieces as
"sudden nests of comfort
amid the modern hustle"
and said they "invite
solid thinking".

②
Atelier Sérgio Rodrigues, Botafogo
Take a seat

Brazil's furniture industry owes
a great deal to the late Sérgio
Rodrigues. "While Brazilian
architecture was known worldwide
during the 1950s, interior design was
always Bauhaus," says his widow
Vera Beatriz. "Sérgio changed that by
incorporating into his design a native,
indigenous Brazilian way of living."

You can buy pieces here –
including the iconic Poltrona Mole
armchair – or just admire his oeuvre:
a virtual collection of designs can
be viewed by appointment. "All he
wanted was to draw; he was alienated
from the sales part," says Beatriz.
Rua Conde de Irajá, 63
+55 (21) 2539 0393
sergiorodrigues.com.br

Left a bit...
right a
bit...

①
Copacabana Promenade,
Copacabana
Walk this way

This black-and-white stone mosaic
is as much of a marvel as the iconic
strip of sand that runs alongside it.
Designed by Roberto Burle Marx,
the promenade was inspired by the
19th-century mosaics inlaid in the
streets of Lisbon. The design of long,
continuous waves – echoing the
lapping sea nearby – was completed
in 1970 and stretches the 4km length
of Copacabana Beach.
    Those staying at a grand suite at
the Fasano (*see page 20*) have a bird's-
eye view from their balcony of a bold
additional design by Burle Marx: a
series of stylised interlocking loops on
the pavement along Ipanema Beach.
Both designs have become poetic

hallmarks for each neighbourhood
– you'll see the patterns printed on
tourist trinkets across Rio.
Avenida Atlântica

②
Snack kiosks
Beach emblems

Rio's seaside kiosks are not
just an essential pit-stop during
any trip to the beach but also
integral elements of the city's
coastline. They range in form
from the sleek curved-glass
models on Copacabana Beach
designed by Indio da Costa
to the older and more scruffy
establishments on Ipanema
and Leblon. They serve drinks
(including beer) and assorted
snacks. Keep an eye out for
those with fresh coconuts.

The mosaic
led to this
deckchair –
what was
I to do?

Street sweepers
Spotless reputation

Wherever you go in Rio your path will cross some of the city's unlikeliest heroes: its omnipresent binmen, or *garis*. Dressed in luminous orange, they traverse the city at most hours of the day and night by truck, van and foot.

Perhaps the most famous of the street sweepers is Renato Sorriso who was filmed one year during the clean-up of the Rio Carnival dancing an elaborate samba routine with broom in hand. The footage made Sorriso a star in Brazil (*see page 83*) and his newfound career as a dancer reached its pinnacle in 2012 when he performed at the closing ceremony of the Olympic Games in London.

Bike Rio
Wheel deal

The bright orange bicycles of Rio's public-cycling system were launched in 2011. There are 60 stations and some 600 bikes to be found around the city. The cost of renting one is a mere R$10 for a month's access. The bikes themselves are a little sleeker in their design than their counterparts in London or Paris.
mobilicidade.com.br

Volkswagen Kombis
Camper-van craze

Up until December 2013 Brazil was home to the last Volkswagen Kombi factory in the world so this 1950s relic is still a common sight. Cherished by Cariocas, it's also a reminder of the importance of good design and reliability.

Marca RJ branding campaign for entrepreneurial spirit
Brand conscious

When it was confirmed that the city would host two of the sporting world's most prestigious events (the Olympics and key World Cup games), it was forced to consider what "Brand Rio" actually is. In 2011 the state government enlisted the help of Brazilian agency Prole to develop a fitting emblem for the city's entrepreneurial spirit.

The result was Marca RJ, a fuss-free all-white logo. Inspired by the registered trademark symbol, it plays an important role in a campaign dedicated to celebrating the heritage of the state. "Marca RJ was not only owned by the government, but it was a mark of the Rio citizen," says Fabiano Pinheiro, Prole's art director for the project.

While the campaign's lifespan is all but over, the RJ can still be seen embossed on shopfronts, skateboards and cars. Just a few of the businesses that bear the sign are the womenswear brand Farm, Zazá Bistro and CT Boucherie.

Sport and fitness
—— Health kicks

Rio is a city unashamedly obsessed with looks and this means Cariocas are constantly exercising: cycling, running, working-out, paddling and swimming. Luckily the city's breathtaking natural surroundings, improving infrastructure and favourable weather create an almost perfect formula for an active lifestyle.

Following extensive consultations with Rio's active crowd we've compiled the following pages to help immerse you in this avid fitness culture.

Runners can pound the pavement on over 8km of sandy shoreline, players can join beach *futevôlei* matches and adrenaline junkies can cycle rugged trails through Parque Nacional da Tijuca. There's also swimming, paddle-boarding and Brazilian jiu jitsu. And if you're in need of a massage or some grooming, we've listed our favourite spots.

The early bird
——
Before the shoreline is besieged by beachgoers and hordes of vendors there's a tranquil period just around dawn; this is when Cariocas sneak down for their daily dose of fitness. You'll spot volleyballers, surfers, runners and more hopping to it under the rising sun.

①
Beach futevôlei, Ipanema
No hands allowed

The legend of *futevôlei's* beginnings varies depending on who you ask but it is an undeniably Brazilian pursuit. Every afternoon from 17.00 Rio natives take to Ipanema's sandy courts and strike up a game of this seamless combination of football and beach volleyball.

You and your teammate have a maximum of three hits to propel the ball over the two-metre-high net, all while playing on the calf-stretchingly soft sand. One more thing: you can't use your hands.

If you're confident head straight to the beach for the evening pick-up games. If not, book a lesson with national champions Eduardo Gasparini and Marcello Schilling. In between playing – and winning – pro tournaments, these childhood friends run training clinics for *futevôlei* doubles.
Ipanema Beach
+55 (21) 992 972 087
eduardinhoemarcellinho.com.br

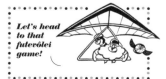

Let's head to that futevôlei game!

Football teams

For a football-loving foreigner going to Maracanã Stadium to see a classic derby match might seem like a once-in-a-lifetime event. However, for many Cariocas it's more of an every-Sunday occurrence – and they're fanatically devoted to their clubs. Here are Rio's top four you need to know about.

01 Fluminense: This was the first club established in the city in 1902 and is known as "Tricolor". It's considered the team of the elite (although you will see all types among its ranks). Its main rival is Flamengo.

02 Flamengo: By far Brazil's biggest football club. You will most definitely spot these black-and-red shirts during your visit and the fanbase is notoriously loud.

03 Vasco da Gama: Founded in 1915 by Portuguese immigrants, the club became well known for paving the way for a more inclusive football culture when it refused to comply with a ban on black and mulato players.

04 Botafogo: This team is known affectionately as *A Estrela Solitária*, or "The Lone Star", due to its badge. Its number seven shirt has been worn by some of the biggest names in the game.

②
Hiking Dois Irmãos, Vidigal
On the up and up

An hour's trek will see you to the summit of the taller of the mountains known as the Two Brothers, which sit at the end of Leblon Beach and are synonymous with Rio's skyline.

To reach the trail take a taxi to Vidigal then a van or a motorbike to the top of the favela. Don't be alarmed by the word "favela": Vidigal is a vibrant community popular with young families, artists and expats. However, we do recommend you avoid hiking alone.

The 1.9km-long trail weaves through rainforest, breaking occasionally to reveal sweeping views. Awaiting you at the peak is arguably the best panorama of the city.
Avenida Presidente João Goulart

③
Brazilian jiu jitsu, Tijuca
Throw down like a local

In the early 1900s the chief of the Japanese immigration colony Esai Maeda befriended a Brazilian named Gastão Gracie. Maeda shared his love of martial arts and, as the story goes, Gracie shaped the ancient fitness form into what is now known as Brazilian jiu jitsu. Since then it has become a cult sport in Rio.

Gracie Tijuca is run by Vinicius Aieta, who was trained by the Gracie family and remains true to traditional techniques. His lessons also take place on one of the largest training mats in town.
*Gracie Tijuca, Clube AABB,
Rua Hadock Lobo, 227
+55 (21) 8795 6354
gracietijuca.com.br*

④
Paddle-boarding,
Copacabana
Balancing act

When it's calm the waters of
Ipanema and Copacabana fill with
the silhouettes of stand-up paddle-
boarders. Eduardo Laucas and his
father have been operating their rental
tent, Sup Copa, from Copacabana
Beach since 2009. "I fell in love with
stand-up paddling the moment I tried
to stand on one," says Laucas.

Hire options cover 30 minutes or
an hour, while lessons in the protected
waters of Posto 6 are also available
for beginners. You can paddle along
the length of the shoreline as no
restrictions exist on where boards
can venture.
Posto 6, Copacabana Beach
+55 (21) 998 282 566

Outdoor gyms
Hit the beach

Life's a beach
—
Outdoor
recreation
reigns in
Rio

①
Rio Academia, Ipanema
Free and easy

You'll notice Rio's shoreline is dotted
with free outdoor gyms. Here,
brawny bronzed bodies hoist chins
over bars and Lycra-clad legs pump
furiously on elliptical machines.

In addition to these permanent
fixtures, further equipment is
installed every summer as part of
the Rio Academia programme run
by NGO Arte e Vida and funded
by the government. These pop-
up open-air gyms on Astroturf
offer weight-training and cardio
equipment and classes include
capoeira, pilates and tai chi. Be
sure to check seasonal hours
and locations.
Ipanema Beach
rioacademia.com.br

Circuito da Praia, Flamengo
All class

If the weather is in your favour – and there's a good chance it will be – then do as the locals do and take your fitness regime to the great outdoors with a circuit class. The team at Circuito da Praia will put you through your paces on the sands of Flamengo and Botafogo beaches. All equipment is provided for the circuit- and resistance-training sessions. We recommend the Flamengo Beach outpost as it offers a more flexible timetable and is bordered by green space Aterro do Flamengo. Bookings are essential.
Flamengo Beach
+ 55 (21) 991 458 520

How many more until I look like these guys?

More beaches
It would be remiss of us to publish a guide to Rio de Janeiro without conducting the tough task of researching the best beaches that you can visit. Travel southwest out of the city and you'll find a number of calm, beautiful stretches away from the usual hotspots.

01 Grumari: Head here on a weekday and you'll come across a near-deserted, pristine expanse devoid of the city's regular hustle. As it's in a municipal park buses can't enter, so book a taxi for the one-hour drive from Zona Sul.

02 Prainha: A strong undercurrent rules Prainha Beach out in terms of a leisurely dip (for that you can drive five minutes to Grumari) but it's where you'll find the serious surfers. The breathtaking backdrop of Pedra Branca State Park alone is worth the trip from the city.

03 Joatinga: A short trail down a rocky inlet and you'll find yourself on Joatinga Beach in Joá. The clear green waters are cradled beneath towering rock faces creating a dreamy setting for a dose of sunshine and salty air.

04 Praia da Reserva: This near unspoilt beach (Avenida Lucio Costa runs parallel) is part of a 20km-long golden expanse near Barra da Tijuca. Conditions are ideal for both swimming and water sports but no vendors operate here so it's best to pack a picnic.

Swimming
Take a dive

①

BodyTech, Barra da Tijuca
Ticking all boxes

With 16 outposts citywide
a BodyTech gym is never more
than a short jog away, offering
air-conditioned respite when the
weather is too steamy to exercise
outdoors. In operation since 2005,
the brand is known across the
country for its modern, immaculately
kept fitness centres. Alongside the
well-stocked rooms of treadmills and
weights, most of the locations also
feature a swimming pool and spa.

The Shopping Cittá branch
is the largest in the city and has
a spa and gymnasium; the
five-lane indoor pool is ideal
for chasing the black line. Single
day passes are available at all
BodyTech locations.
Avenida das Américas, 700
+55 (21) 2132 7222
bodytech.com.br

②

Swimming club, Copacabana
Hitting the open water

It's little surprise that lap pools
have failed to catch on in this
geographically blessed city.
Instead, every morning Olympic
triathletes and recreational
swimmers alike complete laps of
the bay off Copacabana Beach.

Open-water swimming poses
some risks so play it safe and join one
of the clubs that operate from the
beach. Natação no Mar Copacabana,
run by former Olympic swimmer
Luiz Lima, hosts training sessions
every Tuesday and Thursday
morning from 07.00 to 10.00. Phone
ahead to book a session suited to your
abilities as routes vary.
Posto 6, Copacabana Beach
+55 (21) 9872 1754

Horseracing

Arguably one of the most
scenic racing tracks in the
world, Rio's Jockey Club is
worth the outing if only to
see its backdrop. The grand
colonial entrance opens onto
a track boasting the lagoon in
the foreground and towering
hills behind

A rather casual affair, races
take place every half hour on
Friday and Monday from 18.00
and Saturday and Sunday
from 14.00. Bypass the
grandstands and book a table
on the terrace of Rubaiyat
(*see page 36*). Or for a night
on the tiles, join the younger
generation at the charming
Palaphita Gávea bar.

Cycling routes
On your bike

①

Leblon to São Conrado
Cycling route

STARTING POINT:
1114 Avenida Delfim Moreira
DISTANCE: 5.6km
The government has invested heavily in pedal power in the past two decades, building over 450km of cycle lanes and helping to fund more than 600 orange Bike Rio bikes. Perhaps the most scenic and impressive infrastructure to emerge for cyclists is the new two-metre-wide cycle lane that hugs the rugged coastline south of the city.

Hire your Bike Rio wheels from the docking station at ❶ *1114 Avenida Delfim Moreira* and head out towards the coast. Enter the cycle path just off Avenida Niemeyer. Pass the ❷ *Sheraton Rio* outpost and cycle below the Vidigal neighbourhood nestled into the walls of Dois Irmãos. Just past Posto 13 you'll pass the ❸ *São Conrado Beach Club* on your right. If your legs are growing heavy, head a little further along to the ❹ *1400 Avenida Prefeito Mendes de Moraes* to dock your bike, or return the way you came.

②

Circuito do Açude, Parque Nacional da Tijuca
Cycling route

STARTING POINT: Estrada da Cascatinha
DISTANCE: 3km
You'll need a well-equipped bike, a helmet and some off-road experience to tackle this ride through the Parque Nacional da Tijuca. Bike & Lazer in Ipanema or Special Bike in Copacabana can fit you out with rental gear and the staff will provide additional tips about the trail upon request.

Start pedalling on the shared trail that runs off Estrada da Cascatinha near ❶ *Restaurante Os Esquilos*. The track soon turns into a bike-only zone, weaving and bobbing toward ❷ *Rio Humaitá*. After a short rest continue on until the track ends and ❸ *Rio Solidão* converges with the road. This is the approximate halfway point, but the remainder of the journey is along a road (be mindful of the occasional passing car) that heads back to the starting point.

Neymar learned all his moves from me

Haircare and grooming

Cariocas are grooming junkies; Rio's beauty industry is the fastest growing worldwide. Nail salons, plastic-surgery clinics, dermatologists, hair salons, teeth-whitening centres and cosmetic-product retailers are sprouting all over the city. Here are our picks of the finest spots to ensure you're suitably turned out for Rio.

01 Jacques & Costa Barbearia e Chopp, Laranjeiras: A reliable choice for a beard trim. The snug chairs and crisp beers make it hard to leave.
+55 (21) 2532 6683

02 Care Body & Soul, Ipanema: This full-service spa has a good hair studio and its beauticians and masseurs offer tanning, waxing and manicures.
salaocare.com.br

03 Copacabana Palace Spa, Copacabana: One of the most exclusive spots for indulgence. Treatments use organic products made from Brazilian ingredients such as açaí, guaraná and Amazonian white clay.
belmond.com/copacabana-palace-rio-de-janeiro

04 Alex Viana, citywide: To smooth the niggles of a long-haul flight or relieve aching muscles book a shiatsu massage. Viana will stretch and mobilise you.
+55 (21) 997 156 003

05 Bruno Donati Estúdio de Beleza, Jardim Botânico: Bruno Donati is a third-generation Italian hairdresser. Sit in his chair for a skilled cut and maybe an opera tune or two from the man himself.
brunodonati.com.br

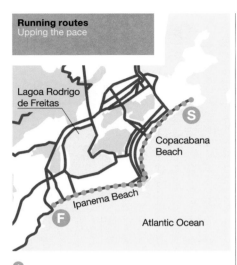

Running routes
Upping the pace

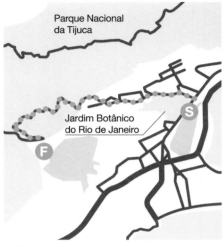

①

Leme to Leblon
In the thick of it

DISTANCE: 8.2km
GRADIENT: Flat
DIFFICULTY: Hard
HIGHLIGHT: The hustle of the beach
BEST TIME: Late afternoon on weekdays

Although some may argue that the route along Copacabana and Ipanema beaches is best left alone during peak exercise hours, there's no denying that it's a hive of energy. As the intensity of the sun weakens, the shoreline thrums with punters keeping fit, whatever the method. Understandably this might deliver some obstacles in maintaining a steady pace, so to ease you into this collective mass begin the run in the quieter northern pocket of Leme Beach.

Follow the stretch of black-and-white tiles and head south toward Copacabana to run the full stretch of the two neighbouring beaches. Near the end of Copacabana at Posto 6 you'll see paddle-boarders out at sea; this will also be the location for the Olympic triathlon swim.

Veer away from the beach and then follow Rua Francisco Otaviano around to your right to run the short distance from Copacabana over to Arpoador. A further 100 metres down the road, take a swift detour through the small, skater-filled Parque Garota de Ipanema: you'll emerge onto the pedestrian path of Arpoador Beach.

Carry on along Ipanema past the *futevôlei* matches and football nets, passing over the Jardim de Alah Canal. The waterway is lined with trees and separates Ipanema from Leblon. Pick up pace and run all the way to the end of the path, where the tiles stop and the red bike-track loops around a tree – the signal to end.

②

Vista Chinesa
Forest beauty

DISTANCE: 5.5km
GRADIENT: Uphill
DIFFICULTY: Hard
HIGHLIGHT: The rewarding view from the top
BEST TIME: Early morning or afternoon

This route will take you around the outskirts of Jardim Botânico, a vast tropical ecosystem, then into the shaded sanctuary of Parque Nacional da Tijuca. Bear in mind that this run follows the 5.5km-long road up to the Vista Chinesa with some very steep inclines so it's not for the faint-hearted – but the view from the top is worth every bead of sweat.

Start at the northeast corner of Jardim Botânico on the corner of Rua Jardim Botânico and Rua Pacheco Leão. Run up Pacheco Leão passing Rua Corcovado to your right where you'll see La Bicyclette, a great French bakery and café (*see page 29*). Keep beneath the shade of the trees and continue on. Just under the 1km mark the garden grounds will come to an end and you'll feel a very slight gradient kick in. The houses to your left will temporarily drop away, hidden behind a graffiti-festooned wall and a dense throng of vegetation.

This is your cue to cross the road before the footpath disappears. When you reach the fork in the road, veer right along Estrada Dona Castorina and steel your legs for the steep incline past the final cluster of houses before you enter the national park. Be wary of passing traffic as you soak in the fresh air and enjoy the native vegetation, including trumpet trees and giant carinianas.

Once you emerge triumphantly at the top after the seemingly endless winding trail, head onto the viewing platform to look back down on your journey. For your return either phone a taxi or run the 5.5km back; at least it will be downhill all the way.

③
Botafogo to Flamengo
Beach and views

DISTANCE: 7.6km
GRADIENT: Flat
DIFFICULTY: Medium
HIGHLIGHT: Watching the sun rise across the bay
BEST TIME: Early morning

This run begins at Praia Vermelha in Urca and travels north along Guanabara Bay away from the ocean. Begin your workout at the cable-car station that ferries customers up to Sugarloaf Mountain. Head northwest, finding your rhythm along Avenida Pasteur, towards Botafogo Beach. You'll pass the Rio Yacht Club on your right, shortly followed by Fogo de Chão, one of Rio's best barbecue restaurants with incredible views of the mountain.

The scenery will open up as you run around Botafogo Beach on the footpath that borders the sandy inlet. Continue along this track until you reach Parque Brigadeiro Eduardo Gomes across the road on your left. This is your opportunity to catch your breath and take in the modernist Museu Carmen Miranda.

Once you're ready, continue on. You'll pass the pyramid-like statue of Espaço Cultural do Monumento Estácio de Sá, which was erected in 1973 in honour of the city's founder. Duck to your right along the dedicated running path and away from the main road. Continue on past Flamengo Beach to Marina da Glória. This is the official Rio de Janeiro 2016 Olympic Games sailing location.

Close to your final destination, you will see the impressively large Second World War memorial on your left. Begin your warm-down as you approach the shady solace beneath the Museu de Arte Moderna (*see page 92*). Walk underneath the museum and head out to the main road to hail a taxi if you need one.

④
Lagoa Rodrigo de Freitas
Lakeside escape

DISTANCE: 7.5km
GRADIENT: Flat
DIFFICULTY: Medium
HIGHLIGHT: The changing skyline
BEST TIME: Late afternoon on weekdays

A simple yet rewarding run, this will take you on a loop around the picturesque Lagoa Rodrigo de Freitas. The 7.5km-long lane that circles around the lake behind Ipanema Beach is busy with joggers and cyclists in the early evenings. It's a good idea to follow suit and avoid the blazing daytime heat but for safety reasons don't head here after dark.

There's no specified starting point for this run so begin at the most convenient entry point for you. Follow the path that circles the lake. You'll pass stalls offering *água de coco* (coconut water) and cafés selling snacks. Foot traffic frequently draws to a standstill as onlookers gaze over at the helicopters landing opposite the Jockey Club and watch the Botafogo Rowing Association train its Olympic hopefuls on the water.

Bar Lagoa (*see page 30*) on the southern bank serves some of the best *pastéis* (savoury pastries) in the city while about 600 metres east the palm-roofed bar Palaphita Kitch (*see page 40*) offers punchy caipirinhas. Both options are well-deserved post-run rewards.

Where to buy
—
Our top picks for running gear in Rio de Janeiro: Brazilian brand Track & Field's (*tf.com.br*) outpost in Leblon and Nike Brand Experience (*nike.com*) in Ipanema.

Walks
— Find your own Rio

Rio's neighbourhoods run the gamut from the glamour and style of Ipanema to the stately, slightly neglected charms of Santa Teresa. Each has something unique to offer but you need to really dive in to discover them. So we've provided you with guided routes around five districts to help you get up close and personal.

NEIGHBOURHOOD 01

Jardim Botânico
Lush city haven

Considering the lush tropical vegetation and the occasional *mico sagui* (small native primate) tiptoeing along the power lines, it is hard to believe that the Jardim Botânico district is just a stone's throw away from the city's most densely populated areas. Named after the botanical garden created in 1808 that sits within its boundaries, this small neighbourhood directly under Christ the Redeemer's right arm also encompasses Parque Lage and part of the Parque Nacional da Tijuca, making it exceptionally rich in both fauna and flora.

During Portuguese rule the area around Rua Pacheco Leão, known as Horto, used to house employees of the garden and a nearby gunpowder factory. The colourful street has now become a vibrant culinary hub dotted with delightful bars and restaurants. The residential back streets that climb up Corcovado Mountain are home to fine examples of domestic architecture, chic retailers and art studios. Wander a little further towards the lagoon and you'll come across the headquarters and studios of the mega broadcaster Globo, making the neighbourhood a common stomping ground for *telenovela* stars.

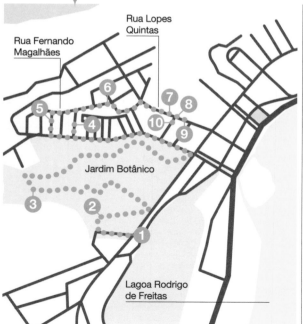

Cafés and green space
Jardim Botânico walk

Begin your walk with breakfast at the charming French bakery ❶ *La Bicyclette (see page 29).* To get there, enter the gates at Rua Jardim Botânico and walk past the colonial mansion to access Espaço Tom Jobim – named after the bossa nova musician – within the grounds. Next to the theatre you will see the bakery.

Buy a ticket (R$9; cash only) and enter the turnstiles into ❷ *Jardim Botânico.* Founded by Dom João VI of Portugal, this garden is considered one of the city's greatest jewels. Find your way to the main pathway Aléia Barbosa Rodrigues, walking alongside the rows of Imperial Palm trees; these were all derived from a single tree planted by Dom João VI himself.

When you reach the fountain turn left on Aléia Frei Leandro. Make your way to the ❸ *Orchidarium* which houses more than 2,000 species of the tropical flower. Exit onto Rua Pacheco Leão and turn left. As you walk, notice the bars and restaurants in the old mansions – they all buzz with life at night.

Turn right on Rua Alberto Ribeiro to find ④ *Isabela Capeto* on the left side of the street. Capeto is a Brazilian designer known for her romantic creations incorporating embroidery. Turn right when you exit and walk back to Rua Pacheco Leão.

Continue along the street, again with the gardens on your left. At the intersection turn right onto Rua Caminhoá. For lovely handmade baby products, pop into atelier-cum shop ⑤ *Família Ripinica*.

Exit and turn right. Walk to the end of Rua Caminhoá and take a right onto the residential Rua Fernando Magalhães, noticing the large detached houses of the neighbourhood, uncommon for Rio. Keep an eye out for *micos* (small primates) on the power lines and trees above. After 200 metres, turn right on Rua Presidente Carlos Luz. Follow until the T-junction with Rua Von Martius; here, on your right, you will find the artisanal atelier and not-for-profit shop ⑥ *O Sol Artesanato*, which produces a range of wicker baskets, bags and hammocks.

When you leave continue walking uphill on Rua Corcovado to the next intersection. Turn right and head downhill on Rua Lopes Quintas. After two minutes you will come to ⑦ *Casa Carandaí* on the right, a pit-stop for snacks or a coffee at the back of the shop.

A further 15 metres down you'll hit ⑧ *Dona Coisa* (*see page 53*), which stocks eclectic womenswear. Continue downhill on Rua Lopes Quintas for another minute. On the same side of the road you will see a black awning over a storefront and a large iron key next to an entrance. ⑨ *Gabinete Duilio Sartori* (*see page 57*) houses design pieces including artisan

textiles and handicrafts made by Brazilian indigenous tribes.

Hungry for lunch? If so, make a left as you walk out of Gabinete Duilio Sartori and walk uphill, taking the first left onto Rua Visconde de Carandaí. ⑩ *Volta* is the second house on your left and serves Brazilian food with flair.

If your energy is still high, exit and make a right, then right again back onto Rua Lopes Quintas. You'll quickly reach Rua Jardim Botânico. Turn left onto it and continue for three blocks. On your right will be Hospital Lagoa, built by the legendary Oscar Niemeyer. Continue for six blocks and you will reach the gates of Parque Lage. Walk in to the main house and art school and relax with a coffee in the courtyard, overlooked by Christ the Redeemer.

Address book

01 La Bicyclette
Espaço Tom Jobim
Rua Jardim Botânico, 1008
+55 (21) 3594 2589
labicyclette.com.br

02 Jardim Botânico
Rua Jardim Botânico
+55 (21) 3874 1808

03 Orchidarium
Jardim Botânico

04 Isabela Capeto
Rua Alberto Ribeiro, 17
+55 (21) 2537 3331
isabelacapeto.com.br

05 Família Ripinica
Rua Caminhoá, 36
+55 (21) 2294 1628
familiaripinica.com.br

06 O Sol Artesanato
Rua Corcovado, 213
+55 (21) 2294 6198
osolartesanato.org.br

07 Casa Carandaí
Rua Lopes Quintas, 165
+55 (21) 3114 0179
casacarandai.com.br

08 Dona Coisa
Rua Lopes Quintas, 153
+55 (21) 2249 2336
donacoisa.com.br

09 Gabinete Duilio Sartori
Rua Lopes Quintas, 87
+55 (21) 3173 8828
gabineteduiliosartori.com.br

10 Volta
Rua Visconde de Carandaí, 5
+55 (21) 3204 5406
restaurantevolta.com.br

Getting there
——
Jardim Botânico can be easily accessed by foot if you are in the neighbourhoods of Gávea or Lagoa. Walking from Leblon would take about half an hour. The area is a short taxi ride from most areas in Zona Sul but be warned: during rush hour traffic can be gridlocked.

NEIGHBOURHOOD 02
Botafogo and Humaitá
Culture fix

Botafogo and Humaitá sit in the centre of Zona Sul wedged between two bodies of water: Guanabara Bay to the east and Lagoa Rodrigo de Freitas to the west. There is no beachfront property here like there is in Ipanema and Copacabana but that's made up for with spectacular views of Sugarloaf Mountain and Christ the Redeemer.

This area is having its moment. Old Portuguese colonial houses are being rejuvenated and some are now World Heritage sites; they're transforming into co-working office spaces, restaurants and entertainment venues. New luxury condo complexes are appearing on nearly every block. And with the resulting surge of trendy independent restaurants and new bars Botafogo is earning itself the nickname "Bota-soho". It's now home to many creative agencies, production studios and mixed-use spaces, and the influx of creatives is making this Zona Sul's new centre of cool.

The small pedestrian neighbourhood of Humaitá sits on the western edge. Named after the Battle of Humaitá in the Paraguayan War, its leafy streets are home to Brazil's International Cinema Academy and provide opportunities to spot Christ the Redeemer.

Even though the two neighbourhoods are considered separate they are pretty much unified. They boast good transport links, cheaper rent prices compared to Copacabana, Ipanema and Leblon, and a less touristy atmosphere than other parts of Zona Sul.

Culture and cuisine
Botafogo and Humaitá walk

Exit the Botafogo metro on Rua Voluntários da Pátria and you'll find **①** *Le Dépanneur* right outside. It's perfect for a coffee or brunch. Next door is **②** *Estação Botafogo*, one of Rio's oldest cinemas. Here you can catch a matinée of the latest international and Brazilian films.

Cross Rua Voluntários da Pátria and go to **③** *Livraria da Travessa*. It's easy to while away hours browsing in this refurbished Portuguese colonial-house-turned-bookshop.

To see where one of Brazil's literary greats once lived take a short walk down Rua Nelson Mandela on the thoroughfare by the metro exit, then turn left on Rua São Clemente to **④** *Fundação Casa de Rui Barbosa*. This museum was home to writer and politician Rui Barbosa, who played an important role in drafting the first republican constitution in Brazil with his liberal ideas.

Mirante Dona Marta has one of the best views in the city of Guanabara Bay and Sugarloaf Mountain. To get there turn right when you exit and make your way up Rua São Clemente; you will see Christ the Redeemer on the hill in the foreground. You will arrive at a small square called Praça Corumbá. This is the base of Favela Santa Marta, which has had a full-time police presence since 2008. The favela view points are accessed by the **⑤** *Plano Inclinado lift (stop 5)*. Guides stand by for any tourists wanting to take a tour of the favela, which is where Michael Jackson filmed "They Don't Care About Us" in 1996. If you prefer you can ask to be taken just to see the views; be prepared for plenty of stairs.

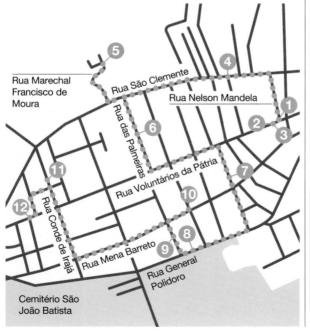

Getting there

Metro lines 1 and 2 connect Botafogo to Zona Sul and Centro. For those heading to the district and its neighbour Humaitá from Sugarloaf Mountain, taxis can also be easily flagged down on Rua São Clemente or Rua Voluntários da Pátria.

After making your way down, **⑥** *Museu do Índio* is less than one block away. Cross to the opposite side of Rua São Clemente away from the square and walk to your left. Turn right onto Rua das Palmeiras and continue for 200 metres or so. The free museum celebrating Brazil's indigenous heritage will be on your left.

Exit and continue down Rua das Palmeiras. Turn left on Rua Voluntários da Pátria and right on Rua Paulo Barreto to reach **⑦** *Zissou Bistrô Bar*. It's run by Argentine chef Eduardo Pretti (who goes by the name Tuna) and the decor is dedicated to the film *The Life Aquatic with Steve Zissou*, making for a quirky happy hour for any Wes Anderson fans.

Leave and make a left, continuing to the T-junction with Rua General Polidoro. Turn right and you can't miss **⑧** *Cemitério São João Batista*. This cemetery is the resting place of nine Brazilian presidents, composers Vinícius de Moraes and Tom Jobim, and architect Oscar Niemeyer. Once a month there are guided tours.

Across the street from the cemetery's entrance on Rua São João Batista you can find **⑨** *Teatro Poeira*. There are performances every night and many of Brazil's Globo actors have transitioned from the screen back to the stage here.

For a few drinks post-theatre (or post-sightseeing) head to **⑩** *Comuna*, a popular bar. To get there, turn left as you exit Teatro Poeira and take the first right on Rua Mena Barreto. At the end of the block turn left onto Rua Sorocaba. The bar is a few steps down on the right-hand side. The no-frills venue also houses a small art gallery and bookshop and its massive burgers have been voted the best in Rio.

If you're after something more refined one of the best meals in town can be eaten 10 minutes' walk away at **⑪** *Lasai* (*see page 31*). Turn left when you exit Comuna and right onto Rua Mena Barreto. Continue for three blocks and turn right at Rua Conde de Irajá. After another three blocks you will have reached Lasai. This Brazilian fusion restaurant in a Portuguese heritage house only opened a few years ago but already has a Michelin star. There's a new menu every night and bookings are essential.

If you are still not ready to call it quits head to **⑫** *Cobal do Humaitá*. Leave Lasai and turn left, then take the first right onto Rua Capistrano de Abreu. Turn left on Rua Marques and right again on Rua Voluntários da Pátria. The entrance is a few steps away. This old tram garage is now a large food market with restaurants and bars, and there is often live samba and bossa nova music. With views of Christ the Redeemer from the patio it's a nice reminder that you're really in Rio.

NEIGHBOURHOOD 03
Santa Teresa
Artistic heritage

Santa Teresa is arguably Rio's most enchanting neighbourhood, characterised by crumbling colonial-style mansions and shaded cobbled streets on a hillside overlooking Guanabara Bay. From the last decades of the 19th century to around the middle of the 20th, this was the haunt of Rio's aristocracy. They built their European-style houses up here to make the most of the cooler, cleaner air and the surrounding greenery.

   The neighbourhood fell out of fashion during the second half of the 20th century as the beachfront districts of Copacabana and then Ipanema grew in popularity. However, Santa Teresa always retained its loyal artistic community thanks to its faded grandeur and scenery. In the past decade it has once again risen in the estimations of Cariocas and visitors alike.

   Some of the city's best hotels, both large and boutique, are to be found here; there are excellent options for eating and drinking, and the artists and designers based in the area ensure things stay lively. Anyone with an eye for colonial architecture or ancient transport (a Lisbon-style tram still trundles up and down the streets), or simply wanting a break from the hustle, bustle and heat of the city, should find a wander around this neighbourhood a wonderfully novel experience.

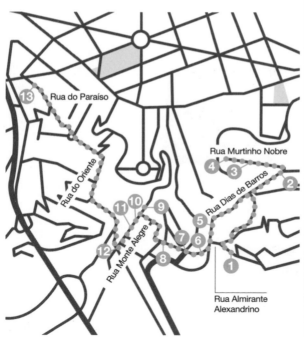

Rua do Paraíso

Rua do Oriente

Rua Murtinho Nobre

Rua Dias de Barros

Rua Monte Alegre

Rua Almirante
Alexandrino

Artisan goods
Santa Teresa walk

Start early with a modern Brazilian breakfast of tapioca omelette, French bread and homemade jam on the veranda of Jean Michel Ruis's boutique hotel ❶ *Mama Ruisa* (*see page 22*), down the cobbled street of Rua Santa Cristina. Call ahead to reserve a table as bookings are essential. After breakfast walk up the hill and take a right on Rua Candido Mendes, then immediately veer left onto Rua Bernardino dos Santos. Turn right on Rua Dias de Barros. At number 47 you'll find the atelier of visual artist ❷ *Atelier Zemog*; again, you'll need to call ahead to arrange a visit but it's well worth it. Zemog himself will show you around and explain the stories behind each of his colourful pieces.

   Continue up the hill and peel off up Rua Murtinho Nobre where you'll spot ❸ *Parque das Ruinas*, a park and art gallery built around the ruins of a mansion that once belonged to aristocrat and patron of the arts Laurinda Santos Lobo. The beautiful building is now owned and managed by the city and is open from Tuesday to Sunday, 10.00 until 20.00.

   Continue further up the road until you reach ❹ *Museu da Chácara do Céu*, which has a collection of European art (including works by Picasso, Seurat and Matisse) as well as plenty of pieces by Brazilian artists.

   Having perused the collection you should have built up an appetite. Head back down to Rua Dias de Barros (continuing on as it changes to Rua Almirante Alexandrino) to ❺ *Espírito Santa*. We recommend

one of the seafood dishes inspired by the northeastern state of Bahia.

Next, wander a few doors down to the charmingly cluttered handicrafts shop ⑥ *La Vereda*, where you'll find everything from paintings and tapestries to lamps and furniture. From here it's only a few short steps to Rua Paschoal Carlos Magno, home to half a dozen restaurants and cafés packed into a short row of shopfronts. Stop for a caffeine fix (or even a craft beer; it is past noon, after all) at ⑦ *Cafecito*, a cosy café and bar up a flight of stairs set back from the road.

Hopefully now you're feeling suitably refreshed and re-energised. Continue along Rua Paschoal Carlos Magno and poke your head into ⑧ *Tucum*, a shop for artisanal jewellery and accessories from across Brazil that is named after a ubiquitous species of palm tree. Leave the shop and follow the road as it ducks right then left until you reach the T-junction with Rua Monte Alegre. Turn right and you'll soon stumble across ⑨ *Museu Casa de Benjamin Constant*, a picturesque 19th-century mansion where Constant, one of the founders of the Brazilian Republic, lived (and died). It has now been turned into a museum dedicated to capturing the social context of his time.

Retrace your steps and pass the T-junction. On your right you'll

Getting there
—
Santa Teresa is a tricky place to get to on public transport, so we recommend hopping in a taxi and removing the hassle. Driving is also not advised as the cobbled roads – while picturesque – are narrow and windy and often a nightmare to navigate.

see the ⑩ *Centro Cultural Laurinda Santos Lobo*, an exhibition space and concert venue in another historic mansion. Forty metres further on you'll come across ⑪ *Atelier Ana Durães*, a Rio artist known for her striking portraits. You'll now be within striking distance of Santa Teresa's most popular *boteco*, ⑫ *Bar do Gomes*, where you can grab a drink and soak up the lively atmosphere.

From here you can either call it a day or squeeze in one more stop. Jump in a taxi or walk for 15 minutes to ⑬ *Atelier Ricardo Fasanello* (*see page 116*) on Rua do Paraíso. To get there on foot turn left on Rua Áurea then right at Rua do Oriente, following it as it turns into Rua Progresso. At the roundabout take Rua Pintora Djanira and then you'll see Rua do Paraíso on your left. Dip down the hill and head for number 42 (call to check if it is open). The mid-century furniture designer, arguably best known for his Esfera armchair, used this space as his atelier but it also houses the workshop where a small number of pieces are still produced.

(*see page 116*)

Address book

01 Mama Ruisa
Rua Santa Cristina, 132
+55 (21) 2508 8142
mamaruisa.com

02 Atelier Zemog
Rua Dias de Barros, 47
+55 (21) 988 885 719

03 Parque das Ruínas
Rua Murtinho Nobre, 169
+55 (21) 2224 3922
rio.rj.gov.br

04 Museu da Chácara do Céu
Rua Murtinho Nobre, 93
+55 (21) 3970 1126
museuscastromaya.com.br

05 Espírito Santa
Rua Almirante Alexandrino, 264
+55 (21) 2507 4840
espiritosanta.com.br

06 La Vereda
Rua Almirante Alexandrino, 428
+55 (21) 2507 0317
lavereda.art.br

07 Cafecito
Rua Paschoal Carlos Magno, 121
+55 (21) 2221 9439
cafecito.com.br

08 Tucum
Rua Paschoal Carlos Magno, 100
+55 (21) 2242 5860
tucumbrasil.com

09 Museu Casa de Benjamin Constant
Rua Monte Alegre, 255
+55 (21) 3970 1168
museubenjaminconstant.blogspot.com

10 Centro Cultural Laurinda Santos Lobo
Rua Monte Alegre, 306
+55 (21) 2215 0618

11 Atelier Ana Durães
Rua Monte Alegre, 301
+55 (21) 996 210 079

12 Bar do Gomes
Rua Áurea, 26
+55 (21) 2232 0822
armazemsaothiago.com.br

13 Atelier Ricardo Fasanello
Rua do Paraíso, 42
+55 (21) 2232 3164
ricardofasanellodesign.com

NEIGHBOURHOOD 04
Lagoa to Ipanema
Beachside saunter

The story of Ipanema and its transformation into the most glamorous address in Rio can be told through two songs. The first is "The Girl from Ipanema" ("*Garota de Ipanema*"), first released in 1962 and written by two of Rio's most famous sons: Tom Jobim and Vinicius de Moraes. It tells the story of a young girl who the duo spotted walking past the Veloso bar one morning. The song captured the spirit of the neighbourhood in the 1960s: vibrant, artistic and carefree.

The second song was written in 1972 and composed by De Moraes and celebrated songwriter Toquinho. *Carta ao Tom* (*A Letter to Tom*) is a love letter of sorts that expresses nostalgia for the days before the views of Christ the Redeemer to the north were blocked by high-rises and the artists who gave the neighbourhood its heartbeat were priced out. "Do you remember those times?" de Moraes asks in the song. "Ipanema was just happiness."

Ipanema today continues to boast some of the highest property prices in Rio. But its quiet, leafy residential streets dotted with charming cafés, restaurants and boutiques mean it is still one of the most romantic and fashionable corners of the city.

Beach culture and bossa nova
Ipanema to Lagoa walk

Begin at Rua Nascimento Silva, 107 which is referenced in the song *Carta ao Tom*. It's dedicated to Tom Jobim who lived here in the 1950s and wrote songs including *Desafinado* and *Samba de uma nota só*.

Facing the building, turn right and walk down Rua Nascimento Silva. Take the first right on Rua Vinícius de Moraes and walk three blocks until you reach ❶ *Lagoa Rodrigo de Freitas*. Cross Avenida Epitácio Pessoa and walk east along the lagoon. You can take a ride on one of the swan-shaped pedaloes on the eastern edge. When you get back to land stop off at ❷ *Palaphita Kitch* (*see page 40*) for a caipirinha or a fresh coconut.

Walk back where you came from and join Rua Vinícius de Moraes once again. This time head south and take the third right onto leafy Rua Barão de Jaguaripe. Keep walking along the quiet canopied street. You'll notice that many of the trees have orchids strapped to their trunks, a wonderful decoration created by the doormen from the apartment buildings there.

On the second block on the left-hand side of the road, stop in at ❸ *LZ Studio*, a shop with pieces by Brazilian and international designers. When you exit turn left, then take the first left on Rua Maria Quitéria. Walk south to the end of the block, turning right back onto Rua Nascimento Silva. Continue along for one block, then turn left onto Rua Garcia d'Ávila and walk towards the beach. After three blocks you will arrive at the intersection with Rua Visconde de

Pirajá. On the corner is a bronze statue of ❹ *Luis Lopes*, a fabled figure in Brazil's War of Independence with Portugal. Legend has it that on 8 November 1882 during the Battle of Pirajá the commander of Brazil's battalions ordered his troops to retreat. Lopes, a bugler, disobeyed and played the call for the troops to charge. Brazil went on to defeat the Portuguese in a pivotal battle.

If you're peckish pop across the intersection to ❺ *Kikarnes* supermarket and pick up a *sonho*: a small doughnut filled with either creamy custard or *dulce de leche*.

Wend your way east from the intersection along Rua Visconde de Pirajá, Ipanema's main shopping thoroughfare. After three blocks, take a quick detour by making a left onto Rua Vinícius de Moraes to find the wonderful ❻ *Toca do Vinícius (see page 58)* record store. Charismatic owner Carlos Alberto Afonso will be happy to give you a history lesson on bossa nova, the genre born in Ipanema.

Turn right as you leave and take the first left to continue walking east on Rua Visconde de Pirajá. After two blocks, turn right onto Rua Teixeira

de Melo. Pop into ❼ *Praça General Osório* on your left, a square that is packed with market stalls selling everything from little hand-carved models of Christ the Redeemer to T-shirts and antiques.

Continue south on Rua Teixeira de Melo and one block after the park you will reach Avenida Vieira Souto, the street that runs along the beach. Take time to admire ❽ *Casa de Cultura Laura Alvim (see page 100)*, a cinema and cultural centre a few steps to the right. Then cross to the other side of Avenida Vieira Souto to reach the promenade and turn left.

No gentle meander along Ipanema would be complete without stopping at one of the drink-and-snack huts. A green coconut with a straw will set you back just R$5. After a five-minute stroll you will arrive at the statue of treasured songwriter ❾ *Tom Jobim*. Take a moment to soak in the view that stretches before you along the beach, with the dramatic Dois Irmãos Mountains in the background.

Facing the beach, walk to the left until you reach ❿ *Arpoador Inn.* Try to bag a table outside for cooling caipirinhas at sunset. There are always street artists playing bossa nova on their saxophones or acoustic guitars.

Next, walk along the beach towards Dois Irmãos. The promenade was designed by the landscape architect Roberto Burle Marx. Dinner at ⓫ *Zazá Bistrô Tropical* is a 10-minute stroll away (six blocks from the Tom Jobim statue) along Ipanema Beach. Cross over Avenida Vieira Souto and enter Rua Joana Angélica to your right. At the end of the block you will see the restaurant, which serves largely Asian fare; revive with seafood noodles.

Getting there
——
Rua Nascimento Silva in Ipanema is a short walk from the neighbourhoods of Leblon and Lagoa. If you are coming from Centro, you can take Metro Line 1 and walk from Praça General Osório.

NEIGHBOURHOOD 05

Centro to Lapa
The heart of the city

The story of Rio de Janeiro begins in the area known simply as
Centro where Portuguese soldiers pushed out the French defenders
and their indigenous allies in 1565. The symbol of Portugal's victory
– a fort atop the Morro do Castelo, or Castle Hill – does not exist
anymore: the entire mountain was bulldozed in the late 19th and
early 20th centuries in response to the then widely held belief
that it spread disease in the city below by impeding airflow.

Walking through Centro to Lapa can feel like leafing
through the chapters of a book; nowhere else in Rio are
the stages of the city's history so clearly defined. There is
a wealth of architectural styles on display, from the colonial Paço
Imperial (once home to the Portuguese royal family seeking refuge
from Napoleon) to the floridly neoclassical Theatro Municipal.
The conical Catedral Metropolitana São Sebastião is a bold
example of the concrete movement that came to characterise
Brazil's urban centres from the 1960s onwards.

With its liberal peppering of *botecos*, trinket shops and samba
spots in nearby Lapa, Centro is a rarity among commercial and
administrative hubs – it's full of life.

Stroll through the ages
Centro to Lapa walk

Begin your walk at the imposing neo-
gothic ❶ *Igreja da Candelária*, which
was built as a chapel in 1634 and
transformed into a cathedral in 1898.
The ceiling panels inside painted by
João Zeferino da Costa depict the true
story of a Spanish merchant and his
wife, who survived a perilous storm at
sea. They erected the original chapel
upon safely reaching dry land.

Next walk along Avenida
Presidente Vargas towards Guanabara
Bay and turn right when you hit Rua
Primeiro de Março. Across the street,
you'll see ❷ *Centro Cultural do Banco
do Brasil (see page 90).* This prestigious
cultural outpost hosts art exhibitions
and was designed by architect
Francisco Joaquim Bittencourt da
Silva, one of the first to link the arts
with education.

Leave the CCBB through the Rua
Primeiro de Março doors and turn
left. Walk south until you arrive at
❸ *Praça XV.* Fable has it this grand
colonial square was built to mark the
landing spot of Portugal's royal family
when they sought refuge in Rio.
Dominating the square is the ❹ *Paço
Imperial* museum which was built
in 1743 and once served as home to
the royal court of Portugal. Be sure
to pop your head into the Arlequim
music shop, which often hosts small
concerts by local musicians.

If you've just snapped up a
Carmen Miranda record, you might
want to head back west across the
square and walk through the famous
Arco do Teles archway to ❺ *Travessa
do Comércio*, a narrow cobbled
street of colourful *sobrados*
(colonial townhouses). The
legendary Brazilian songstress

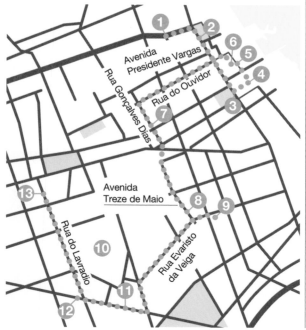

lived at number 13 before Hollywood beckoned.

If it's lunchtime get a table at the recently opened ❻ *Restaurante Bastião* and sample Brazilian fare. Next, walk away from the archway and turn left on Rua Do Ouvidor, then left again on Rua Gonçalves Dias to ❼ *Confeitaria Colombo*. Opened in 1894 as a bakery, it became a favoured haunt of Rio's intelligentsia, among them the poet and children's writer Olavo Bilac.

Leave Colombo, turn left and then continue on the pedestrianised Rua

Gonçalves Dias; cut through Largo da Carioca square. On the far right you will spot the brutalist Petrobras building (its headquarters) and soon arrive at the ❽ *Theatro Municipal*. This elaborate building was styled after Charles Garnier's Paris Opera.

If you have time to kill before the evening's performance, cross the street to the magnificent ❾ *Biblioteca Nacional*. This incredible 200-year-old space is home to approximately 10 million books, making it the largest library in Latin America.

Getting there

The Igreja da Candelária is located a short walk from Uruguaina metro stop on one of Rio's busiest thoroughfares – Avenida Presidente Vargas. Several bus routes run through here but the easiest way to get around is to simply hail a taxi.

From here head to Lapa, looking out for the concrete cone of the ❿ *Catedral Metropolitana de São Sebastião* (*see page 104*). Skirt around the southern edge of the cathedral and make your way toward the grand ⓫ *Arcos da Lapa*, otherwise known as the Carioca Aqueduct (*see page 115*). As you cut below the arches look back for an impressive view of the skyline. Next, walk alongside the archway up Avenida Mem de Sá until you reach Rua do Lavradio. On your right-hand side, just after the crossroads, grab an ice-cold *chope* at ⓬ *Bar Brasil*, an institution that opened its doors in 1907 and has been serving Brazilian and German fare ever since.

Once you've drained your glass head back to the intersection, this time turning left to walk along Rua do Lavradio and stopping in at some of the design stores along the way. Every first Saturday of the month this strip becomes a popular antique market known as "Feira do Rio Antigo". If you're in the dancing mood, continue for just a few minutes more and end your walk at the famous ⓭ *Rio Scenarium* dance hall.

Address book

01 Igreja da Candelária
Praça Pio X
02 Centro Cultural do Banco do Brasil
Rua Primeiro de Março, 66
+55 (21) 3808 2020
03 Praça XV
Praça XV de Novembro
04 Paço Imperial
Praça Quinze de Novembro, 48
+55 (21) 2215 2093
paçoimperial.com.br
05 Travessa do Comércio (Carmen Miranda's house)
Travessa do Comércio, 13
06 Restaurante Bastião
Travessa do Comércio, 11
+55 (21) 2224 8602
07 Confeitaria Colombo
Rua Gonçalves Dias, 32
+55 (21) 2505 1500
confeitariacolombo.com.br
08 Theatro Municipal
Praça Floriano
+55 (21) 2332 9191
theatromunicipal.rj.gov.br
09 Biblioteca Nacional
Avenida Rio Branco, 219
+55 (21) 2220 9484
10 Catedral Metropolitana de São Sebastião
Avenida Chile, 245
+55 (21) 2240 2669
catedral.com.br
11 Arcos da Lapa
Carioca Aqueduct
12 Bar Brasil
Avenida Mem de Sá, 90
+55 (21) 2509 5943
barbrasil.com.br
13 Rio Scenarium
Rua do Lavradio, 20
+55 (21) 3147 9000
rioscenarium.com.br

Resources
—— Inside knowledge

So you've been discovering the ins and outs of Rio de Janeiro: you can weave your way around a samba dance floor and you're up to speed with beach etiquette. Here you'll find out the best way to get from A to B, get a quick lesson in Brazilian Portuguese and learn about the city's iconic soundtrack. Our events calendar will keep you in the know and our weather-proof tips will take care of you come rain or shine.

Transport
Get around town

Rio de Janeiro's public transport greatly improved after the city was awarded the 2016 Summer Olympics, although it's still far from perfect. Here's how to get around.

01 Metro: Line 1 and Line 2 will take you around Zona Sul (South Zone), downtown and into parts of Zona Norte (North Zone). Line 4, which will have stops in Gávea and Barra da Tijuca, is being built in time for the Olympics. Each trip costs R$3.70; metro cards can be bought at any station.
metrorio.com.br

02 Bike: Bike Rio is a bike-share system that can be signed up for online and paid for by card. It costs R$10 a month or R$5 a day. Bike stations are throughout the city.
mobilicidade.com.br/bikerio.asp

03 On foot: Walking is the best way to take in Rio's sites but with temperatures sitting at 40C in the summer months it's not advisable to be outside around midday. After dark, take a taxi for safety.

04 Private cars: Enquire at your hotel to ensure the best rate and a trusted driver. Most only speak Portuguese.

05 Taxi: Yellow cabs can be flagged on nearly every corner. For safety, taxis are often called using apps such as *99Taxis* and *Easy Taxi*.
99taxis.com/en; easytaxi.com

06 Flights: Rio de Janeiro has two airports: Santos Dumont for domestic flights and Rio de Janeiro International Airport (known as Galeão). Leave plenty of time to get to Galeão as traffic can be unpredictable.
infraero.gov.br; riogaleao.com/en

07 Helicopter: Head to the Parque dos Patins in Lagoa to catch a one-hour panoramic chopper ride over the Cidade Maravilhosa.
helisight.com.br

Vocabulary
Local lingo

01 Bom dia: Good morning
02 Boa tarde: Good afternoon
03 Boa noite: Good night
04 Beleza: All good
05 Carioca: Local resident of Rio
06 De nada: You're welcome
07 Lindo(a): Beautiful
08 Obrigada: Thank you (for women)
09 Obrigado: Thank you (for men)
10 Oi: Hi
11 Por favor: Please
12 Tchau: Good bye
13 Tudo bem? How are you?

Soundtrack to the city
Five top tunes

01 Vinícius de Moraes and Tom Jobim, 'The Girl from Ipanema': This 1962 number is one of the most-performed songs in the world. The track still paints an accurate picture of Ipanema's beautiful people.

02 Tim Maia, 'Do Leme ao Pontal': This fun 1980s classic describes beautiful Copacabana from start to finish.

03 Gilberto Gil, 'Aquele Abraço': Called "That Hug" in English, this iconic samba song celebrates Rio's people and famous Carnival.

04 André Filho and Aurora Miranda, 'Cidade Maravilhosa': This oldie but goodie was composed in 1935 and people have been referring to Rio as the "Marvellous City" ever since.

05 'Imaginario, 450 Janeiros de Uma Cidade Surreal': Written for the Portela samba school by its in-house composers, the 2015 Carnival theme tune takes you on a tour through Rio and pays homage to the people of Madureira.

Best events
What to see

01 Carnival: Between the street parties (*blocos*) and the parade at the Sambadrome there is no shortage of partying during the world's largest street festival.
February or March, rio-carnival.net

02 Rio Open: This tennis tournament is in its infancy but it is the only combined ATP 500 world tour and WTA event in South America.
February, rioopen.com

03 Rio Content Market: The region's biggest movers and shakers in film and television meet to speak about audiovisual content.
March, riocontentmarket. com.br

04 É Tudo Verdade: International documentary film festival that takes place every year in Rio de Janeiro and São Paulo.
April, etudoverdade.com.br/ br/home

05 ArtRio: This international contemporary-art fair gets bigger and better every year.
September, artrio.art.br

06 Rock in Rio: South America's largest music festival has been going strong for 30 years. Expect national and international artists.
See rockinrio.com/rio for dates

07 Book Biennial: One of Brazil's most important literary events, this international book fair takes place every two years.
September, bienaldolivro. com.br

08 Festival do Rio: An annual film festival that brings the very best of international cinema to the country.
October, festivaldorio.com.br

09 Gay Pride Parade: This parade is smaller than São Paulo's but it's more scenic: it starts at Copacabana and ends at Ipanema at sunset.
November, gaypridebrazil.org

10 New Year's Eve: Celebrations on Copacabana Beach are among the best in the world.
December

Rainy days
Weather-proof activities

With at least one week of rain each month in Rio it's a good idea to have a few wet-weather options up your sleeve.

01 Museu de Arte do Rio: Opened two years ago, this art museum was part of the Porto Maravilha project to rejuvenate the rundown port area. Half of the building is new and it links up to Palacete Dom João, an early-20th-century palace. It's easy to spend the whole day weaving your way through the exhibitions, which change every few months. Admission is free on Tuesdays.
museudeartedorio.org.br/en

02 Spectator sports: There's no better way of making the most of a spot of wet weather than by joining the crowds at a football match in Maracanã Stadium or watching a race at the Jockey Club. The metro will take you straight from Ipanema to the Maracanã where you can buy your tickets on the day (at entrance A); a ticket costs between R$40 and R$80. A taxi is the easiest way to get to the Jockey Club in Lagoa where entrance is free – though you'll probably want to have a flutter.
maracana.com; jcbinforma. com.br

03 Go shopping: Retail therapy is a sport for Brazilians and fully air-conditioned, US-style shopping centres can be found in every district of Rio, especially in Barra da Tijuca where Avenida das Américas is lined with them. Head to Botafogo Praia Shopping for stunning views of Sugarloaf Mountain and Guanabara Bay from its food court. Or try the quirky Siqueira Campos, one of Rio's very first shopping centres, where you can pick up original crafts and intriguing antiques.
botafogopraiashopping.com.br

Sunny days
The great outdoors

From beaches to mountains, Rio's outdoor riches are many and varied. The activities are plentiful too; here are our top picks.

01 Ipanema: This is where Cariocas go to see and be seen. Between the bronzed and well-toned bodies, the buskers and the food and bikini vendors, a day at Ipanema will give you a good idea of what it means to be a local. To get the authentic experience, go on a Saturday.
ipanema.com

02 Parque Nacional da Tijuca: This lush green space is right in the middle of the city and is the largest rainforest in any urban area in the world. There are a number of trails, including hikes up to the Dois Irmãos and Pedra da Gávea mountains, as well as Christ the Redeemer. You can book a tour or go it alone but be sure to stick to the trails, which are well marked. Dress for the weather, bring plenty of water and sunscreen and avoid walking during the midday heat.

03 Jardim Botânico: Rio's botanical garden was founded in 1808 but began some centuries before as a Portuguese colonial palace where medicinal plants were cultivated. Today it celebrates Brazil's biodiversity (it's home to more than 8,000 plant species) and has been under environmental protection since 1995. It's open every day and the fee is R$9 (cash only).
jbrj.gov.br

04 Head out of town: There are plenty of places just outside the city that are worth a visit, from the fishing village of Búzios to Angra dos Reis, where you can hop between tropical islands. You can also scuba dive off the Ilha Grande and roam the cobbled streets of historic Paraty.

Olympics
—— Navigating the Games

Rio de Janeiro was awarded the Olympic and Paralympic Games in 2009. Between 5 to 21 August 2016 some 10,500 athletes from more than 200 countries will descend on the city to compete for medals. The Paralympic Games will follow, taking place from 7 until 18 September.

The Games organisers have designed the competition to show off the best Rio has to offer, both in terms of culturally significant settings and sheer natural beauty. The opening and closing ceremonies will take place in the newly renovated Maracanã Stadium, for instance, while the salt-water lagoon Lagoa Rodrigo de Freitas and Copacabana Beach will host a variety of sporting events.

Just two years after the city hosted the football World Cup, much of the key infrastructure is already in place. However, several large-scale projects were set in motion in the run-up to the Olympics, including a major plan to revitalise the city's port area, called Porto Maravilha.

Practical information
How to plan your trip

Transport
The Olympic Village will be in the Barra Zone in Rio's west. A number of transport lines will take visitors to the different Games Zones. To get to the Barra Olympic Village from Galeão Airport take the BRT Transcarioca direct. Rio's metro will be running from Centro and Ipanema to the Maracanã Complex Games Zone.

Tickets
01 A total of 7.5 million tickets will be sold (200,000 fewer than 2012, due to smaller facilities than London).
02 Ticket prices range from R$40 for many events to R$4,600 for the most expensive seats at the opening ceremony.
03 For non-Brazilian residents, tickets can be purchased from a list of authorised ticket resellers listed on the Rio 2016 website *rio2016.com*. Ticket sales will be conducted via a system of draws.
04 For Brazilian residents, tickets are available to purchase direct from the website.
05 Tickets not purchased during the draws will be available online on a first come, first served basis.
06 In June 2016, Rio 2016 Games box offices will open and remaining tickets will be available for purchase.

Non-ticketed events
01 Street events can be watched for free.
02 Some sections of sports will be able to be seen without a ticket (such as the road-cycling race and triathlon competitions), although the best way to guarantee a complete view is to buy a ticket.

New sports for 2016
There are two open spots for new sports for these Olympics, with the IOC voting on a number of propositions. The winners were:

01 Golf (individual, no teams)
02 Rugby sevens

Venues
Overview

The Rio 2016 venues are clustered into four Games Zones.

Zone 1: Barra Olympic Park
This is set to be the centre of the games. It contains the Riocentro with its four pavilions, the Olympic Golf Course and the Pontal (for road cycling and the race walk).

Barra Olympic Park
01 Carioca Arena 1: Basketball
02 Carioca Arena 2: Judo; Greco-Roman wrestling; freestyle wrestling
03 Carioca Arena 3: Fencing; taekwondo
04 Future Arena: Handball
05 Rio Olympic Arena: Artistic and rhythmic gymnastics; trampoline
06 Maria Lenk Aquatics Centre: Synchronised swimming; diving
07 Olympic Tennis Centre: Tennis

08 Olympic Aquatics Stadium:
Swimming; water polo
09 Rio Olympic Velodrome:
Track cycling

Riocentro Pavilions
10 Pavilion 2: Boxing
11 Pavilion 3: Table tennis
12 Pavilion 4: Badminton
13 Pavilion 6: Weightlifting

Zone 2: Deodoro
The second Olympic Park will host equestrian events and BMX biking, plus fencing and rugby sevens. It will be home to an extreme-sports park that will remain after the Games, along with the whitewater canoeing course and BMX track.

Deodoro Olympic Park
01 Youth Arena: Basketball; modern pentathlon
02 Deodoro Stadium: Modern pentathlon; rugby sevens
03 Olympic Equestrian Centre: Equestrian dressage, eventing and jumping
04 Olympic Hockey Centre: Hockey
05 Olympic Shooting Centre: Shooting
06 Deodoro Aquatics Centre: Modern pentathlon

X-Park
07 Mountain Bike Centre: Mountain bike
08 Olympic BMX Centre: BMX cycling
09 Whitewater Stadium: Canoe slalom

Zone 3: Maracanã Complex
The Maracanã Stadium will host the opening and closing ceremonies plus football matches, while the Sambadrome – the home of Rio's Carnival parade – will be the start and finish of the Olympic marathon.

Maracanã Complex
01 Júlio de Lamare Aquatics Centre: Water polo
02 Maracanã: Football; opening and closing ceremonies
03 Maracanãzinho: Volleyball
04 Olympic Stadium: Athletics; football
05 Sambadrome: Athletics (marathon); archery

Zone 4: Copacabana
Copacabana Beach will have competitions almost every day, notably beach volleyball. The Games Zone also includes the neighbourhoods of Lagoa (rowing and canoe sprint) and Glória for the sailing competitions.

Copacabana
01 Beach Volleyball Arena: Beach volleyball
02 Lagoa Stadium: Canoe slalom; rowing
03 Fort Copacabana: Road cycling; marathon swimming; triathlon
04 Marina da Glória: Sailing

Branding and font
01 The Rio 2016 logo was designed by Brazilian brand specialists Tátil and unveiled in 2010. Its logo, which beat 138 other agencies in competition, represents three figures in the shape of Sugarloaf Mountain, joined at the arms and in the colours of the Brazilian flag.
02 The Rio 2016 font was created by Dalton Maag, a London-based font studio. It comprises 5,448 characters, with the curve of each letter said to represent the joyfulness of Cariocas.

Mascots
01 The official mascots of the 2016 Rio Olympics, Vinícius and Tom, were announced in 2014 by brand director Beth Lula.
02 Vinicius is named after the late musician Vinícius de Moraes, a master of bossa nova. Tom, the Paralympic mascot, is named after Tom Jobim, another renowned Brazilian bossa nova musician.
03 The mascots are intended to reflect the diversity of Brazil's culture and people.
04 The names were decided by a public vote.

Culture and festivals
01 The Rio 2016 culture programme, dubbed Celebra, is set to host a number of free open-air events in the run-up to and during the Olympic and Paralympic Games. The schedule will encompass music, literature, theatre, dance and visual arts. There will also be a food festival, a sports-film exhibition, urban installations and a musical about Rio.
02 In the run-up, the Rio 2016 Organising Committee has set up a number of festivals to promote Olympic sports to residents. The first was in November 2014 and had 400 people participating in different sports at Games Zone venues. Look out for more such events on the Rio 2016 website.
rio2016.com

Writers
Mikaela Aitken
Matt Alagiah
Fernando Augusto Pacheco
Donna Bowater
Josh Fehnert
Christopher Frey
Georgia Grimond
Tomos Lewis
Gaia Lutz
Claudia Moreira Salles
Carlota Rebelo
Sheena Rossiter
Saul Taylor
Andrew Tuck

Chief photographer
André Vieira

Still life
David Sykes

Photographers
Jacob Langvad
Eduardo Martino
Lianne Milton
Tuca Vieira

Illustrators
Satoshi Hashimoto
Tokuma
Hans Woody

Monocle
EDITOR IN CHIEF & CHAIRMAN
Tyler Brûlé
EDITOR
Andrew Tuck

The Monocle Travel Guide Series: Rio
SERIES EDITOR
Joe Pickard
CITY EDITOR
Matt Alagiah
ASSOCIATE EDITOR
Amy Richardson
RESEARCHER
Mikaela Aitken

DESIGNERS
Kate McInerney
Sam Brogan

PHOTO EDITORS
Renee Melides
Poppy Shibamoto

PRODUCTION
Jacqueline Deacon
Dan Poole
Sonia Zhuravlyova
Chloë Ashby

CHAPTER EDITING

Need to know
Sheena Rossiter

Hotels
Matt Alagiah

Food and drink
Matt Alagiah

Beach business
Matt Alagiah

Retail
Matt Alagiah

Things we'd buy
Gaia Lutz

Essays
Matt Alagiah

Culture
Saul Taylor

Design and architecture
Matt Alagiah

Sport and fitness
Mikaela Aitken

Walks
Matt Alagiah

Resources
Sheena Rossiter

Research
Joey Edwards
Grace Lee
Aidan McLaughlin
Paige Reynolds

Special thanks
Alex Bueno de Moraes
Paul F
Lee Gale
Mariana Mauricio
Claudia Moreira Salles
Fernanda Salem

We hope you have found the Monocle travel guide to Rio de Janeiro useful, inspiring and entertaining. There is plenty more to get your teeth into: our London, New York, Tokyo, Hong Kong, Madrid, Bangkok, Istanbul and Miami guides are on the shelves as we speak, with Paris and Singapore joining them in the coming months. Cities are fun. Let's explore.

01
London
The sights, sounds and style of the British capital.

02
New York
From the bright neon lights to the moody jazz clubs of the US's starring city.

03
Tokyo
Japan's capital in all its energetic, enigmatic glory.

04
Hong Kong
Get down to business in this vibrant city of depth and drama.

05
Madrid
A captivating city that is abuzz with spirit and adventure.

06
Bangkok
Stimulate your senses with a mix of the exotic and eclectic.

07
Istanbul
Where Asia and Europe meet – with astonishing results.

08
Miami
We unpack the Magic City's box of tricks.

09
Rio
An enchanting city of beaches, bars and bossa nova swagger.